OMG
My God, My God

By

Yusef Harris

B. Global Publishing

OMG! MY GOD, MY GOD

ISBN: 9780988786608
© 2013 B.Global Publishing

B.Global Publishing
6341 Eilerts
Wichita, KS 67218

Printed in the United States of America

OMG! MY GOD, MY GOD

Special Thanks To:

GOD – Jesus Christ – the Holy Spirit through which all things are.

Geno Stinson for your friendship, ear and your advice. Thanks for sparking my OMG moment.

Dr. Thomas Bettis Jr. for your spiritual brotherhood, advice, suggestions and for letting GOD lead you to lead me.

The Harris Family, all of you have made it so very important for me to be the best that I can be, you love, play and live hard and set a level of expectation that requires a high level of virtues to be called a Harris(Immediate and Extended, all generations).

Riccardo Harris, GOD put us together for a reason, divine inspiration is ingenious… Thank you brother.

OMG! MY GOD, MY GOD

Contents

OMG! MY GOD, MY GOD

PREFACE

One day I was speaking to a friend on the phone and the conversation was one that should have taken place much sooner than it did. During the conversation I ended up sharing some advice with my friend, in hopes of helping him repair a relationship in which he was involved. I had tried to have the conversation with my friend prior to his involvement in the relationship, but I was only able to share a few things before he made the decision to be involved.

During our belated conversation, my friend let me know that I had shared a lot of insight and perspective that was really eye opening for him. I had no idea that the information I was providing him would seem so beneficial to him. His comment was "You should write a book." I laughed a little and continued on with the conversation and then I hung up the phone. After I got off of the phone I gave some serious thought to his advice about writing a book. After all, he had just taken the advice I'd offered him, so I thought maybe I should also consider the advice he offered me. As I thought about the possibilities of what he'd said, I had my "OMG" moment.

After my "OMG" moment, I started thinking about the 16 hours in a day that I'm awake and how I was horribly mismanaging them. I could literally visualize every waking moment in my life that I was not being productive and I could see that I was literally wasting my life away, one unproductive day at a time. We all do it.

We just sit around every day wasting time, talent, experiences, and ideas.

We all have a gift or something special about us that makes us unique; that gives us purpose on this earth. Some of us go through life never acting on the "<u>OMG</u>" moment. Perhaps, we've heard motivational speeches or encouraging words from friends that started the creative juices flowing and created that "OMG" moment, but we let procrastination or some minute event in life side track us from greatness or an opportunity to change at least one life.

I remember the phrase *Oh my God!* and its popularity during my teenage years. Sir Mix A Lot capitalized on the phrase in a popular song that I won't mention here.

OMG! MY GOD, MY GOD

You know, it's funny that phrase has managed to survive through the 90s into the age of the World Wide Web and is now a popular abbreviation used on blogs and IM chats. "OMG" has resiliently held a place in popular culture for at least 19 years. So, I thought, "OMG" has got to be the title of my book. It signifies that moment that you realize the power or importance of a situation and expresses your level of unbelief about the realization. It symbolizes the *I can't believe it* moment you experience when you've heard an incredible or unbelievable story about someone or something. "OMG" symbolizes the realization of your true potential to do the things you were put on this earth to do, like making a difference, changing or saving a life or creating the next solution to a global problem. "OMG" represents the moment of clarity that you experience when you finally understand what life's all about. "OMG" is the moment of epiphany, where your thoughts about something are crystal clear; the light is on and something is illuminated.

I realize that throughout life we experience a wide range of emotions and situations that can be life changing and can also affect other people, our views, and our belief system. From a spiritual stand point, we sometimes experience a shaking of our beliefs based upon the reactions to people that we love or care deeply about. As human beings, we sometimes try to function as if we are not part of a larger unit or group. If we think about it, even the animals in nature know that we all must function as part of a larger group. Ants are a perfect example of how individuals responsibly make up a unit, with each individual performing a specific function and

11

taking on certain responsibility so the entire colony of ants can have the shelter and food that they all need as individuals. It's also noted that if one ant is destroyed, the unit carries on their primary functions for a positive end result for the whole colony of ants. As human beings, we do not follow a pattern such as this, and often we don't take a look at how our personal decisions can affect hundreds or even thousands of other people. Most importantly, we do not always stop and think about how our actions will affect our dearest and nearest loved ones.

Even though people are usually happy to talk about their successes, often they are very reluctant to share their "non-successes." For those who attend church, this example will really hit home. In many churches, people are given the opportunity during the meeting time or services to give their *testimony*. This is the opportunity for people to tell how good the Lord or the Creator has been in providing material or financial things, healing someone who was sick or injured or working out a difficult situation in someone's life. Testimony time is a time to tell of the relief of your troubles. When testifying, people will normally only tell about the things that they consider good things. As an example, one might say, "I had a bill due and the Lord provided some money out of nowhere," or "God blessed me with a brand new car." While this is a moving testimony, we will often create the premise that these are the *only* *situations* in our lives. We are happy to proclaim the situations that have a good outcome, but are very reluctant to share our failures in life and what we learned from them. For example, you may rarely or never hear someone say, "I am a habitual liar and I have been delivered from this, and here is how it happened" or "I had a problem with overeating and here's how I overcame that situation." We have difficulty sharing what we consider our "bad" experiences because it's really too embarrassing in a lot of cases. It's usually an admission of sorts that we have done something negative or have been living a negative lifestyle, and we would usually rather keep that to ourselves.

What you may not understand is that there is probably someone else that is struggling through that same type of situation that you've struggled with, and they would really benefit from your experiences. When you speak about your problem, it may help someone else realize that they are not the only person in the world with that problem. Someone who is listening may feel hope rise up in them because they see that you have struggled and overcome, and that means it is possible for them to do the same thing.

In the spirit of these few thoughts, I am making an attempt to follow my friend's advice. I am attempting to share the things that I have learned in my life in hopes that I can reach or help at least one individual in their troublesome time. This book is my way of reaching out and sharing what I know so that it may benefit others. Responsibility starts right here—with me. If I can take responsibility for sharing what I know, maybe the next person can, too. When one person sets a spark, the fire grows and many will be warmed and continue to share the warmth.

In the course of my life, I've had thousands of unrecorded "OMG" moments. I never really acted on most of them. I can't count the many times my eyes have widened and my eyebrows have arched as I've thought "OMG," only to forget about it soon afterward. In other words, I didn't follow through. Life moves fast. We're all busy. Unfortunately, too many of our "OMG" moments come and go without being acted upon.

During the conversation that sparked this "OMG" moment, I mentioned to my friend that I had tried to write a book before, but I had failed to take the time to follow through and finish it. But this time, I did follow through and my "OMG" moment resulted in this book. I

hope it makes you say "OMG" (Oh My GOD) thousands

of times and motivates you to do something about it.

Please enjoy!

OMG! MY GOD, MY GOD

INTRODUCTION

I guess I am finally here. I am finally at a place where I
am no longer procrastinating; where I can freely share
my thoughts, my mind, and my soul, and bear it all, so to
speak, (or at least most of it) one word at a time. I have
experienced so many life-changing situations during my
life, but it took me such a long time to realize that the
decisions and actions that I make can affect so many
other people. Sometimes those people are close to me,
and sometimes those people are emotionally far from
me. No matter, life is a series of events that hinge upon
each other, one day at a time. How we start the day is
often how the day ends up. We often live life on a daily
basis, not thinking about how we are living will affect
our future or affect others. We often don't think of or

expect any repercussions or results. We think we're just living, forgetting that every single thing we do has some impact on someone or something.

I have experienced a lot of situations and conditions in life including poverty, racism, wealth, success, failure, sickness, depression, immaturity, maturity, denial, rejection, unfaithfulness, unfairness, betrayal, abuse, pride and humility. Most of these things have been inflicted and experienced with those that are emotionally close to me, such as family, friends, and loved ones. Many of the people affected by my reactions to these things have been people that I don't even know. They are mainly the people that I see on the streets or interact with in public places or at work. This is simply because we will allow those that are close to us to hurt us and never confront or solve problems within the relationships. We will make everyone and everything around us pay the price of the hurt and pain that is inflicted by those that we are close to. In this book, I will expand on this concept and shed more light on the subject of how I believe we can deal with these situations and turn them into solutions and successes, instead of disasters in our lives.

In a relatively short time, I have realized that we go through life without uncovering the keys to true happiness. We go through life being untruthful to ourselves, and this causes us to live our lives without ever really being happy, but just getting by. We wear masks and paste on fake smiles to disguise who we really are, and to convince people that everything in our lives is perfectly fine. I know many people, including myself, that have been exposed to dramatic situations in life that have either made us hide out or morph into other people. Most of us have confronted harsh realities in our lives and experienced very difficult things. Few people, if any, live lives that aren't difficult in some way. But, we live in a world of great actors and actresses.

I am convinced that some of the people that you know and meet in life are capable of achieving Academy Award performances on a daily basis. There are people that you know that live such a different life at home and away from you, that if you were with them 24 hours a day you would marvel at how easily they have absorbed the jagged life that they live. We need to appropriately address all of these things in our lives and learn how to deal with them and make them successful experiences and not life damaging experiences. In this book, I hope to share with you ways to live a life that is true and authentic. I want to bring you some insight that will help you to be responsible and accountable and manage your life so that you and those around you can be truly happy---instead of just going through the daily motions of life while everyone is hurting and no one is doing anything about it.

OMG! MY GOD, MY GOD

CHAPTER 1: DEATH

Death is generally something that is very hard for us to deal with. It is the end to all means, as we know life on this earth. Death is finality, and is also an unknown factor in our minds. We have no idea when we might die or what happens after we take that last breath. There are some that have a belief and faith in a new life after death. There are some that believe that there is no life after death. There are some that believe that you keep coming back in a different form until you get it right. Death is something that we live in denial about for most of our life. What I mean by that is that we know we must die, but our actions show that we don't accept that because we don't really live life like we are dying every day.

OMG! MY GOD, MY GOD

We often live our lives and treat our relationships like our loved ones will always be here with us, acting as if we can abuse them or take them for granted. When we are children, we do things that disappoint and hurt our parents and loved ones, simply because we do not register an end to a person in our reality. Unless they have had a traumatic experience that makes them think otherwise, most children think their parents will always be around. Children are just learning about life and don't understand the sacrifices that are made so that they can enjoy a comfortable life with food, clothing, and shelter provided at no cost to them. In American schools, if children act up, at most they are suspended and given another chance to receive schooling after a period of time. At worst, the child will repeat the same grade until they get it right. In most cases, they don't understand the value of their education or appreciate that it won't be taken away from them, even when they don't appreciate it. Children in other countries where going to school is a privilege appreciate schooling, but American children often consider it a drudgery.

Most American children don't worry about transportation or how they are going to get where they have to go for school plays or functions because they rely on their parents for everything. If their parents are successful, they make it through childhood without really having to pay attention to death or concern themselves with the responsibility of growing up and taking care of themselves. This is a behavior that steers us away from the reality that there is an end to everything material as we know it. There is an end to

OMG! MY GOD, MY GOD

life. Death is something that is a certainty for everyone. It can't be escaped.

As a parent, it is important to respect the reality of death. If we don't teach our children about death and how to function once we are gone, they will no doubt suffer as adult children, following and passing through the same life corridors as we have. Too often, we protect our children from the reality of death, and we teach them to hide death in the back of their minds. We shelter our children from the thoughts and conversations of death because we view it as something bad. We don't understand death so we just try to ignore it because we have no answer for it. We tend to try and protect our children from the things that we think they can't understand or handle when, in fact, some of our children

are very capable of understanding and accepting the
subject of death whether we think they are prepared or
not. In today's society, our children are being forced to
deal with death and its effects, both mentally and
physically. The age groups of the dying are becoming
younger and younger as violence and disease takes a toll
on the younger generations. There was a time that death
was generally associated with the older generation, but
now tragedy strikes all age groups. There are so many
acts of violence and other situations that are now
affecting generations of a much younger age group. With
the affliction of AIDS and HIV, babies are being
introduced to the world at risk of facing death much
sooner than expected. There is disease, famine, and war
that force children around the world to look death and
the after effects of death right in the face, well before

29

they have even had the opportunity to develop good speech patterns or make a decision on what they want to be in life. It is important that we start taking a closer look at death, and the actions we take that make us a part of premature death for ourselves and others.

I know a lot of adults that just have not yet grown up. Legally, they are adults, but mentally and emotionally they are still harboring the thoughts and actions of children. They are still living life as if they don't have any responsibilities and there are no consequences to their actions. They are hiding realities in the back of their mind, like a child. They are pretending if they do not acknowledge certain things, the things aren't realities. I'm sure we all know someone who rightfully should be supporting themselves, but they still live at home with their parents and let the parents support them. They drive a nice car and own the most advanced technical products like computers, cell phones, and video game systems. Like children, toys are what is important to them and they would rather have toys to play with than take responsibility for their own expenses and life.

In these cases, it seems that the umbilical cord of nurturing has not been cut between the child and the parents. I believe that this type of behavior stems from not dealing with the fact that you will have to have an end to your life. We know this end as death, and as a result we don't prepare our children for it. Instead, we create a false reality that parents and the safety net will physically always be there for them. We shield our children from dealing with the realities of life and death.

We don't force our children to look at death and make a plan based upon this sure given in their lives. Since we don't know where and when death will come, it would seem that there is never a time when death cannot be viewed and contemplated once a person is mentally and physically capable of expressing themselves and developing individual thought.

Another thing that relates to death is our health and eating habits. Over the years, we have developed a tolerance for unhealthy living. Often, when people are chastised about their eating habits or unhealthy habits, I have heard them say "You have to die of something." This is a mentality that suggests that death has become an excuse for irresponsibility. The attitude that we're all going to die someday anyway, so why not toss caution and responsibility to the wind and live it up, has created irresponsible eating that creates obesity and disease. It has created an attitude of indulgence and overeating, all while there are many people who don't have enough food to eat on a regular basis.

We can't speak about death without addressing health. A lot of people, especially men, are very reluctant to visit a medical physician in regards to serious ailments or injuries that can sometimes lead to further health complications or even death. Personally, I can admit that my idea of being a man is that you are tough and that you can overcome any situation or circumstance. This includes a little cut or stub to the toe. Men often feel that they can pick up any heavy object by themselves or do any type of house or car maintenance that needs done.

Men feel they should be able to tackle any other physical task that presents itself, and come out looking like a hero to their wife and daughters. Yes, men tend to prefer not to show a sign of weakness, even if they are hurting physically or mentally, in order to prove to themselves and to others that they are *real men.*

Men try to ignore physical illness and injuries and keep on going. They will not take off from their jobs if they are supporting a family. Men will use the excuse that they have to work to support their family, because we don't rationalize that we will one day face death and leave our families unable to support themselves or look for someone else to do that after we are gone. It is really a spirit of pride that causes us to carry this mentality. I also believe that because of the idea and feeling that we are invincible, that we will ignore the reality that we will have to face death. We tend to push it into the back of our minds instead of acknowledging the fact that we will one day cease to breathe and function with life in our bodies.

It's time for men to change their mentality to encompass using all resources that are available to provide the best support that we can for our family and friends. We must start making life and health a priority so that we can truly live up to the potential that we have as men and can take better care of our families while we are on this earth, and set up support for them for when we leave this earth. I think that once we accept death as a reality in our minds, we will change a lot of the habits that we have developed and will abandon the reckless life behaviors that we have taken on as a society.

OMG! MY GOD, MY GOD

Medicine has been used to help mask and disguise the reality of death. After all, we will take medicine and treatments with the hopes of increasing the days of our lives. The reality is that we will eventually die no matter how long we are able to stretch our days. Today, there is a bombardment of advertisements that promote a way to escape the idea of death. The advertised medications are developed to increase the ability to live with sickness and to continue to add days onto our life spans, with limited advertisement on how to live a better quality life with the finality of death in mind. We continue to build hope in the next miracle pill or the next miracle treatment that will grant us the ability to control how long we live. This alleviates the pressures of actually being responsible to live a healthy life and control the situations that we expose ourselves to. Instead of developing good eating habits and exercising, we have a tendency to indulge in whatever we want to eat and use our time sitting in front of T.V., all the while thinking that if this creates health problems for us, we will just take a pill to take care of it. Well, the pills only go so far and once the side effects settle in, the body is worse off than it was before ingesting the medication. It's a vicious cycle that keeps people from enjoying the quality of life that is usually available when effort is made to stay healthy.

Daily, we create fragmented realities that allow us to abandon responsibility for our actions in relation to ourselves and others. No one on this earth can stop death, so we constantly try to invent ways to prolong death, not really facing the fact that death is inevitable, but we can live quality, healthy lives while we are still here.

During funerals, I have noticed behaviors that suggest that people really don't respect death as a reality. I find that usually the people that display the most hurt are people that never realized that the person they mourn would have to die. This is especially evident with children and those younger than the individual who is deceased. The fact is, we take life and death for granted, not expecting that one day the people that we love will no longer exist in our lives as they do now. Over the course of my lifetime, I have heard and witnessed a lot of tragedies and unexpected losses. The tsunami disasters of 2004 resulted in a massive loss of life, young and old, in disproportionate numbers. To me, this was an

awesome reality that death is inevitable and can come at

any time, whether expected or unexpected. Tragedies

really hurt us because we just don't expect death to

arrive at the moments that it does arrive. We can prepare

for dealing with death by living one day at a time. We

have to realize that by changing our perceptions and

expectations of death we can begin to truly enjoy and

respect life and the ones that we love. We have to change

our habits and lifestyles to reflect the respect of death

and life. We have to look at the way we live, our eating

habits, our health habits, our sexual lifestyle habits, and

the quality of life that we choose. By changing our

educational programs, we can learn to teach and train our

children to be able to deal with life and make the

transition to adulthood, if they are spared to see it. By

doing this, we can also create a better quality of life for
our descendants and loved ones.

CHAPTER 2: MONEY

In talking about money, I have to point out a critical misconception that people quote from one of the most popular books of the world, the Bible. People say that the Bible says that "money is the root of all evil," but this is not an accurate quote. I Timothy 6:10 states, "For the *love* of money is the root of all evil: which while some coveted after, they have erred from the faith, and pierced themselves through with many sorrows."

I emphasize *love* in the text because it is the action towards money that creates the root cause of evil. In this society, it is necessary to have money and be involved in commerce to survive in the economical structure that has been designed. My suggestion is that Timothy did not intend that we should forsake the wise use of money, but that we should not irresponsibly spend and mismanage money. He was also stating that we should not love something material so much that we would do anything to get it. We have placed a disastrous amount of attention and exposure to acquiring money at all costs. Our society glamorizes the attainment of money, and profiles many who have attained excessive amounts of money in their lifetimes or careers. If you turn on the news, or any television program for that matter, you will see a reality that suggests that if you don't have money, you cannot be recognized or glamorized. One example of this glamorized lifestyle is *MTV Cribs*. This show gives the world a look into the glamorized lifestyle of many of today's most popular sports, music, and entertainment stars. We also see many of the rap stars glamorized in videos where they live in million dollar

mansions and drive very expensive cars. Today's media

is all about glamorizing and emphasizing the acquisition

of huge amounts of money.

Television creates shows and sitcoms that invite us into

the homes of families and people who never have to

work or who have extremely successful jobs. Successful

people are usually not portrayed to work or even have to

struggle with the day to day responsibilities of paying

bills or having any financial responsibilities. This lends

children the idea that life should be that way. They come

away after watching T.V. thinking that life should be

easy and they should be able to attain great wealth and

success without working hard or taking steps toward

their goals. Since television is now a common household

item, we are visually influenced by what we see on the television. Sometimes, I like to refer to it as the "Tell Lie Vision," because it portrays so many false images and situations. Our children, and some adults, watch television without being equipped to recognize and separate television from reality. Daily, we absorb these false images and jaded realities and sometimes find ourselves trying to apply these scenarios to our own lives.

We have to learn to be responsible with money and develop priorities that will lead to financial success within our individual lives and family lives. How can we do this and teach this concept to our children? It is my suggestion that we incorporate some financial educational curriculum into our school systems. We must start teaching people how to think smart regarding finances, and not just how to memorize or get by. We have to start preparing people for real life. A few of the most interesting situations that have occurred in America in regards to money are the Enron scandal, the MCI scandal, and the forewarned instability of Social Security for the current generation that is headed for the harsh reality of not having it.

When you look at today's society, you can see how irresponsible and unsuccessful we have been with managing money. Our own government is in debt, and that national debt is a reflection of our individual mismanagement of money. It's comparable to a family environment. If you are raised a certain way, the characteristics of your up-bringing will show up in the habits you have and how you react to things. Now, everyone will react differently as individuals, but the general consensus is that people will fall in line with whatever their surroundings are. Normally, if you have grown up in a family that has had problems with paying bills and keeping basic utilities on, you will find that the children will grow up to take on some of the same characteristics. You can usually trace these negative money management behaviors back to the parents or the leaders of the households. If you look at America as a whole and compare individual households across America you will find that the average household is in debt, and just like the country, doesn't really have a sound plan to get out of debt.

There are people that are successful at managing their funds and money, but you will find that these examples are not being emphasized to the masses or being introduced in academic curriculums. We are not showing monetary responsibility in our communities, and therefore our nation struggles with money and how to use it to our advantage. The mismanagement of money in a family causes material and mental strain on each individual that is a part of the unit. When the parents are irresponsible with money or do not manage it well, it creates hardship for the children. When children are not taught to manage their money, the cycle of mismanagement continues on to the next generation and so forth.

In some communities and cultures, the purchase and attainment of things like cars, clothes, jewelry, and accessories are more important than the future of the family's financial stability. These are the cultures that the *MTV Cribs*, *Pimped Out Rides*, and high priced materialistic videos are focused on. Sometimes we don't realize that it is important to leave a financial legacy to build upon. It's so hard to master managing money, and when you do find someone that can do so, they will usually guard their information so it doesn't benefit others. In some instances, successful people will hide their success so they are not accused of acting like they are "too good" for others.

Credit is now a large part of the money management system in America. Most people use credit in one form or another. Credit can be used to your advantage or to your disadvantage, depending on how you use it. Many people think that they can get by with paying the minimum amount due on their credit cards and accounts and do not understand that it will take them the rest of their lives to pay off the balances that they incur. They just don't do the math, even though they get the information sent to them in their monthly statements and before they use the credit card. There are always unforeseen expenses that come up when you least expect them—car repairs, house repairs, school pictures and other little hiccups that occur in our lives and affect us in our finances. I don't know a lot of households that actually *plan* for these things. We are all aware of the concept of unforeseen and unexpected expenses, as we have seen them all of our lives, and as children we even presented unexpected expenses to our parents when we needed money for things for school or a special event. Yet, we continually let these unexpected events catch us off guard.

I don't know of anyone that has not experienced an unexpected event or known of someone that has not experienced an unexpected event that affects them financially. So why don't we plan for these things? It's not that hard to create a plan to set aside a little money for the things that pop up unexpectedly. Mostly, we don't plan for unexpected expenses because we seek instant gratification and spend our money accordingly. We have no intention of having unexpected expenses, even though we have seen it happen over and over in our lives and have seen the impact it can have on our budget.

Furthermore, we never make a plan to have the means to tackle these problems without letting them affect our overall financial goals. This thinking occurs in every society and at every financial level. It's easy to see that the same faulty behaviors are ingrained in the people that are in charge of our nation's wealth, and we are all affected on a larger scale by them not planning for the unexpected.

Money is directly related to divorce, depression, and the low quality of living that some people experience daily in their lives. It's one of the reasons that people cannot receive adequate and quality health care. Money affects many aspects of our live, physically and emotionally. The love of money is behind many of the motives of people from the poorest nations in the world, to our

American leaders, and those that serve at the United Nations. A lot of decisions that are made in regard to our well being and happiness or sadness in life are based upon the motive of the love of money, which, as mentioned earlier, is "the root of all evil." Unfortunately, when the love of money is the motive behind so many actions, there are consequences that follow. Poor quality of life is one of the severest consequences.

CHAPTER 3: CREDIT

Rightfully so, I have to start this chapter out with the definition for the word *credit*. Funny thing is, there are several definitions for the word, and when I went to look up this word, I found some definitions that you might not expect, before I actually got to the one that I think most people would think of first:

> Credit: 1: Recognition or approval for an act, ability, or quality. 2: An arrangement for deferred payment of a loan or purchase.

These two definitions go hand in hand, really, because your credit (recognition or approval for an act, ability, or quality) depends on your ability to handle an arrangement for deferred payment of a loan or purchase.

OMG! MY GOD, MY GOD

Credit, as we know it, is a system that is set up and designed to allow or disallow you to control your comfort of living. Let's face it, you can have all the money you realistically could care to have, but if you don't establish your credit properly you will never achieve a certain level of attaining the things you want in life. There is a way to predetermine and manage your credit to your advantage, but you must understand how credit works. It is designed to undermine and financially classify you. Based upon their credit score, anyone and everyone that will deal with your credit will be able to determine whether or not they would like to discriminate against you; take a risk on you, so to speak. Your credit score is available to anyone who deals with finances or business. There are some rules to playing the game of credit, and it is to your advantage to know the rules of the game.

The first mistake that most people make in regards to credit is that they do not know how to use credit. It is my opinion that, for success, credit should be used only on a 30-day basis. I do not think it is the wisest decision to purchase anything on credit that you will not be able to pay for completely within 30 days. If you can follow this one rule, you can set yourself up for a path of financial success and reward. Your family will also reap the rewards of your following this rule, if you can instill it in them, too.

The second mistake that people make with credit cards and accounts is making only the monthly minimum payment. Do the math. Take your balance times your percentage rate on your card and add that figure to your balance. On some cards, the interest is going to be compounded daily. If you add that up, you will see that you are not just simply borrowing a certain amount of money from the creditor. In simplest terms, I mean that you are not borrowing $500 and paying $500 back later. This company is in the business to make money off of you, and they loan you $500 and you pay back only $500, they can't make any money off you. If you borrow $500, you will have to pay back the $500 plus all of the interest they charge in order to make money. A $500 loan can easily turn into paying back $700 or more. If you do the math and factor in only the minimum monthly payment, you will see that most of that monthly payment goes to paying interest and fees, and not to reduce the actual loan amount. With this in mind, you can see how long it will take you to pay back the original loan amount, and you will also find out that you aren't paying back the same amount that you borrowed. In some cases, you may actually pay back as much as three times more than what you borrowed if you continue to make the monthly minimum payment. The monthly minimum payment amount is usually fairly small and when you receive your statement, you feel okay about just paying the minimum amount that they have suggested. In the long run, this costs you more than you think. It's best to pay your entire balance every 30 days so you don't have to pay large interest amounts. And whatever you do, don't pay your payment late or you will be charged exorbitant late fees, as well as create a negative credit rating.

OMG! MY GOD, MY GOD

Managing your credit is so important in relation to your quality of life and your pursuit of happiness in America. Managing your credit involves a masterful level of discipline. As Americans with so much instantly at our fingertips, we desire to be gratified immediately. We want what we desire right now. We don't want to wait until we save the money to purchase something. We do not have the patience for that. We look at that as an old fashioned way of doing things. That's the way our grandparents and great-grandparents did things! Usually, the motive for wanting something instantly is to uphold whatever image we have created for ourselves. We want to make people think that we are something that we are not. We go through life acting out in Academy Award performances, financing our theatrical productions as though we can afford to do so. We are too concerned about what people think about us, how we are accepted

by society, and how we are classified in social ranking.

Credit has provided another false reality and opportunity

for us to commit financial suicide. In ignorance, we are

being taken advantage of, and it is imperative that we

seek the knowledge necessary to repair and reverse the

inadequate habits that we have in regards to our credit.

The bottom line is that we all put our pants and skirts on

the same way and take them off the same way at the end

of the day, no matter whether they are $50 pants or

$1000 dollar pants. No matter how much we dress up,

we are still naked human beings underneath, which is the

same way we all came into this world. You can buy

things on credit to mislead people into believing that you

are someone that you aren't, but sooner or later the truth

will emerge. We need to learn to embrace who we are and what we are able to achieve with what we have, so that we do not seek out artificial means to dress ourselves up so that other people think we are something we are not. We must stop thinking that what we can afford isn't good enough, and stop comparing ourselves to someone who may have more because they are in different circumstances than we are. We also have to learn to do without and get by without sometimes. It won't kill a person to not have everything they want right when they want it. We must always keep in mind the things we know are financially true, and remain prepared for unknown financial difficulties and expenses.

There are families that live in constant poverty because of the inability to overcome financial adversity. For generations, they have done the same thing the same way, and it is almost impossible for them to climb out of debt and financial mismanagement unless they make changes in their habits and develop a mentality toward financial freedom. We have got to educate and teach the younger generations to escape the mental and habitual slaveries that we suffer from and pass on from generation to generation.

OMG! MY GOD, MY GOD

CHAPTER 4: SEX

Sex is probably one of the most popular and glorified subjects in America. It is something that we have yet to understand and respect. In my opinion, we probably have suffered from and created many diseases because we don't understand the functions and capacities of sex. We have ignored the fact that, bottom line, sex is an action that is intended for the reproduction and perpetuation of life. While it is enjoyable for most people, it is sometimes abused. Because of the desire for sex, our morals and our actions have been outright despicable in dealing with sex. Every religion has their teaching or belief on the purpose or institution in which sex is condoned. It is of my opinion and belief that sex is something that should be sacred and something that should be respected within the confines of marriage. That is what I believe and what I share in this passage. I know that is something that is easier said than done, and I can also say that, although I have been taught that from a young child, I haven't always respected sex as I should have. My opinion is that once you are involved sexually with someone, you have joined yourself spiritually and emotionally with that individual. Ironically, if you want to get in someone's head and know what they think and how they feel, you can physically achieve that by being sexually active with them. Engaging in sex with another person changes things emotionally for both parties, and changes the way people feel about each other.

OMG! MY GOD, MY GOD

Our society glamorizes and even categorizes people according to how sexually active they are. We have glamorized being sexually active so much that we have created a mentality that says that it is okay to have sex before we are emotionally united and committed to functioning as a unit. How hot of an actress or actor one is, now depends on how sexually suggestive or active you can be on screen. This has turned into a disturbing trend in my community, because it has encouraged women to be much more aggressive in seeking pre-marital sex to prove that they are worthy of a male's attention. Some females have now accepted the standard that it is okay for them to use their bodies, and not their minds, to get what they want. They are selling their bodies to get what they want. This is a very disturbing trend and is almost a complete 360 degree turn of prevalent ideas from when I was growing up. There was a time that being a virgin meant something, and saving yourself for someone you wanted to be with for the rest of your life was important. We now live in the day of the "Baby Mama," and "Baby Daddy," where it is okay to mother and father any guy or girl's children without any intentions for commitment and respecting the family structure that has been set up to help us survive. Now days, it is a rare occurrence for an eligible unmarried man to be able to find a woman to marry who does not already have kids from previous relationships.

Men have begun to embrace the fact that they may have to accept and play the role of a father to children who are not theirs. The standards have changed. I have even heard of and encountered situations where women will even lie to a man and tell him that he is the father of her

child when sometimes she doesn't have any idea who the

father is because she has been so sexually promiscuous.

This has been a huge element in destroying the family

structure and respect for it. How can children learn to

have respect for the family when the mother doesn't

even know who the father of the child is? How can a

child embrace the sanctity of the family when there are

no boundaries that surround the family to protect them?

In the history of America, there are many things that

have been inflicted upon us to destroy the family

structure. One such affliction was the treatment of

women during times of slavery. It is documented that

slave women were raped and forced to become sexually

involved with their masters, which I am sure destroyed

the family structure and respect for the women in those families. These were probably some of the first instances of single motherhood. These types of things have created permanent scars on our past and have been destructive in the man's role in protecting his wife and family. They once degraded the very strands of decency in the hearts and minds of male providers and companions. Most of all, they have scarred the mental and physical minds of women who were respected and cherished during the times of slavery. I do believe that the treatment of women in the past has created some of the behaviors that have been passed down from generation to generation. But we must accept that those things are in our past, and we must not forget that *we now have choices on how we conduct ourselves sexually.* So why is it that we now choose to disrespect our own bodies and sexual nature of our own accord? Why do we place ourselves in situations and environments that foster the idea that women want to be raped or taken advantage of? Why do women and men live out the idea that they can display the very physical attributes that are fruits of their sexual nature and expect for the opposite sex not to be aroused or feel invited to become a part of our sexuality? We are now void of the excuse that we are being forced to have sex, and yet, our society has fostered an idea and acceptance that sex is for everyone and there is no responsibility that goes along with it.

Not taking responsibility for and not respecting the consequences or results of sex with multiple partners has initiated some of the negative situations that we see in our society today. AIDS is one of the greatest epidemics that we have experienced over the past 15 years. Because of the irresponsibility and lack of education regarding the results of promiscuous sex, we have created an epidemic. AIDS has been called a man-made disease, which, in itself, is horrible and atrocious, but to continue to perpetuate the epidemic with careless sexual activity is senseless.

There is an underlying cry for us to return to being responsible for our actions and learn to be true to ourselves. We have to emphasize the realities of sexually transmitted diseases. We now have to start educating our children at earlier ages about the dangers of sexual activity at an age that they should be more concerned about playing, learning and growing. As a father of two girls, I am concerned with the necessity of emphasizing and illustrating what can possibly happen to them if they are sexually active at a young age. More importantly, since HIV can have an incubation period of up to seven years, they must be concerned with the possibility that the person they decide to be involved with could be carrying the HIV virus. I shiver sometimes to think of the things that my children will have to think about as they grow up and become adults.

We have to learn to understand sex from a mental standpoint as well. There is a mental effect that sex will have on each individual. Our children are being introduced to sex and sexual behavior at too young of an age, before they are prepared to deal with such mature matters. When children are introduced to sex before they are mature enough to handle it, the results are disastrous.

OMG! MY GOD, MY GOD

We live in a society that is full of child pornographers and pedophiles. In many instances, our children are not safe because people that have been molested are now adult molesters. We cannot continue to shirk the responsibility of addressing signs and symptoms that make us aware that our children are being introduced to sex too early. Once a child is damaged with sexual misconduct, it will affect his or her interaction with other children, and if not addressed, it will affect their childhood, teenage years, and their transition to adulthood.

We have witnessed many sexual scandals and situations in our nation, and it is my belief that the people involved were introduced to sex at the wrong time in their lives or without the proper guidance to mentally understand the effects of sexual activity. Abusers have been abused, and we can't deny that fact. Everything that we know, we have learned from a source that is traceable. The unfortunate thing is that this happens far too often and people that are politicians, entertainers, sports figures, teachers, church members, and prominent community figures are now functioning in our community without the proper help to overcome the damage that has been inflicted on them because of sexual misconduct. We have to, once again, address these issues and take the responsibility to correct these situations.

Sex has gotten so far away from being a spiritual and sacred act that we now have to deal with the consequences of the *abuse* of sex. It is important that we respect sex and hold it sacred, because we will be forced to respect it if we continue on the path of irresponsibility that we are on now.

Once again, in conjunction with the love of money, the love of sex has gotten man into some pretty deep trouble. This confirms the dangers of loving or being obsessed with anything that is material. Naturally, you would have to be inclined to believe that our love should be for things that are spiritual, in order to achieve true happiness in life. In these times, we cannot take for granted that the people that we are involved with will be truthful and not hide the negative things of their past. It could cost you your life to make such an assumption that the person you are involved with is completely honest with you. It is horrible to grip the real thought that your first date should be to a health clinic so that you can get everything out on the table and up front between you and a relationship partner. Now, this is almost the only way to ensure that you are at least on the right track to ensuring a successful relationship.

We have to start talking about these things in more public forums and in private forums. Parents have to take more responsibility in knowing where their children are and protecting them at all times. Most importantly, we can't just stick our children in front of the television as a means of babysitting because they are now being bombarded and targeted to see images of premarital sex and unnatural relationships. Parents must be a positive example for their children so the children can develop a natural and positive attitude about sex, instead of following after what they see on T.V. or in others' lives.

Babies are raising babies, and they have no idea of the perils that can so easily beset our children's futures, because they have not completely passed through the phase of being children and successfully transitioning into adulthood. Young mothers and fathers just don't have the experience necessary to protect their children from the dangers that are lurking to destroy them. As a society, there are so many messages that we send, and we do not realize that those messages are understood by our children much more clearly than we think. The misunderstanding of sex has become a vicious and destructive part of our reality. Just like anything in this world that is mismanaged, immature and mismanaged sexual activity has destroyed the success of families, the dreams of individuals, the lives of human beings, and the healthy and productive Biblical command to be fruitful and multiply. If we don't take the necessary responsibility to restore all natural things, we are accelerating the destruction of creation.

It is necessary for us to repair all of the mistakes we have made. In order to fix the problem, we must recognize and agree that there is one. Next, we must create reachable goals to help deal with the issue of sexual misconduct. Today there are plenty of consequences and horrors that should help to motivate us to think about a social change in regards to sex.

Our children and families are being destroyed because we are not educating our children about the responsibility that comes along with sexual behavior. We are not emphasizing the rewards to being sexually responsible. We are not sacrificing the few minutes of pleasure in exchange for a lifetime of opportunity. So, we must begin to accept the challenge of telling our stories and sharing our experiences with responsibility in order to give our children a fighting chance for a happy, healthy, and successful future.

CHAPTER 5: RELATIONSHIPS

Relationships are special. Relationships are bonds between people or beings. Mostly we think of relationships in regards to intimacy, but when we really think about it, we have a relationship of some sort with just about everyone that we consistently come into contact with in our lives. There are various types of relationships and various levels of relationships. It's important for us to know the value of each one of our relationships and not to be so flippant about our relationships.

Our spiritual relationship, I think, is the most important. This relationship affects what you believe, how you are influenced, and what motivates you in all other relationships. I can only speak from my own experience on what I believe to be my spiritual relationship with God, directly in relation to Jesus Christ. Sometimes, in our spiritual relationship, we fail to realize that it is important for it to be just as personal as any other relationship that we have with any human being. In order to develop a relationship with a human being, I must talk to that person and be able to share experiences. This lets me know what we really have in common and provides an opportunity for me to strengthen my relationship with this person based upon the things that we have in common. In the spiritual sense, we have a form of communication that is allowed and encouraged with our spiritual Creator. That conversation is prayer and meditation. Prayer provides an opportunity for one to express his or her feelings on a situation, seek help, confess, or show and express gratitude towards that person. When you look at it, it is no different than the conversations that we hold with our dearest friends and loved ones. The more comfortable you are with a person, the more uninhibited you can be, and the more honest your conversation is. So we need to realize that in order to express ourselves freely and be completely at peace with what we say in prayer, we have to develop our relationship with God to one that is strong and one that is tried.

Our conversation and experiences are really how we build relationship with one another, and the more we know about each other, the closer we feel to each other. Sometimes we can really learn a lot about a person by speaking to the people who are around that person every day, or by reading about a person. In hearing about a person from someone else, you get a different perspective and are enlightened about the habits and characteristics of the person. In order to develop our relationships with our Creator, we must read about him through other people's experiences. We must talk to people about him. Now, realize that every experience that someone else has may or may not be a good one in their opinion, but you must have the wisdom to discern the truth and good out of the situations that you hear about. Let's face it, we have all heard other people's takes on people we knew and it was not anything like the person we knew. For an example, I have had people to tell me that someone I knew was an inconsiderate person or that they were rude in regards to a famous athlete. I happened to be with that person during a similar incident and just happened to know that that person may have been late or may have had a prior engagement or may have had something on his mind that he was preoccupied with. The story that was told by the other person was that he was rude and he wasn't a very good guy, because the person didn't get what he wanted, which was an autograph. So because this person didn't get things the way he wanted them, his opinion wasn't a nice one. We sometimes do this in regards to our Creator. If things don't go the way we want them to, our report or experience can sometimes be labeled a bad experience.

In regards to God's conversation with us, we will find recorded on several occasions that God spoke to people in the Bible. I am convinced that God speaks to us through his word (the Bible) and also through his Spirit. Many people have proclaimed to hear the voice of the Lord in these days and times and down through the ages. So, we know that he talks to us and through us. Sometimes we are reminded or encouraged to follow the voice of God by the words that may be spoken by an individual who has no idea of the impact of the words they are speaking. The witness of God's conversation to us is real and can be attested to by those who hear his voice through whatever means that he uses.

There are relationships within the family, starting with the husband and wife. This relationship is very important because it directly affects the other members of your family unit. What your children accept or allow in their lives is mostly based upon the communication structure that you develop in front of them. Being in a marital relationship is not much different than being in a spiritual one. You must still have open lines of communication to attain the same goals of creating a bond that can be strengthened as time goes by. Most of the time, the mistake that we make in relationships is ending the communication when we don't agree on something. This is so wrong that I can't stress it enough: you have to keep communication open and ongoing through all processes. The communication must be verbal and physical.

Now, most of the time, people like to argue or become violent to attempt to communicate with each other. This is not the correct procedure for healthy communication. Think about it. If you really want to resolve an issue or difference between you and another person, the first thing you should do is to understand where they are coming from. To overcome your adversity, you have got to learn to put yourself in the other person's place. That means you must drop all preconceived notions and ways of thinking, and get into the vision of the other person involved. There are so many factors that affect the way we think and why we think what we think. Everyone understands things differently, but it is when we can understand or come to a common understanding that we can share ideas on the same level. Think about the word *relation*, meaning to relate, and the word *ship* meaning a quality or possessing a quality. When you put those two words together you get, *possessing a quality to relate.* So, you can check the success of your relationship with your significant other by asking yourself if you have a quality to relate to each other. It's not asking if you have a quality to *agree* with each other. Now, it's good when you can agree, but when you can relate, you can either understand why you don't agree and try and adjust your approach to accommodate, or you can understand why you can't agree. Let's face it, in relationships between men and women, a common failure is that we spend too much time trying to understand each other's differences rather than understanding that we are different. This statement is in relation to male and female genders. We are shaped different and made different, so wouldn't it make sense that we *are* different? Now, I believe that we should all be treated fairly and equally in regards to well being and treatment in the general world, but we don't always think the same way. Respecting and understanding that is a first step to a healthy relationship between man and woman.

Once you understand this principle, you will understand that how you treat that person in front of your children will directly shape the qualities your children will unknowingly reach out to and embrace as they develop relationships with different people. They learn so much from your example and how you do things.

You have also got to be honest with yourself. Every relationship is based on a level of trust and truth. If you don't have trust in a relationship, you can't develop it. If there's no trust, you exist in a conversation and that is it. When you trust someone, really trust them with everything, you will give them everything. That means that your deepest darkest secrets you will share with someone that you can trust on that level. We live in layers of truth. If we trust a person enough, we continue to share a purer truth as our relationship with each other gets deeper and more trustworthy. In order to trust someone, you have to practice trusting that person. When a mother sends a young person to the store to get something for her, she usually sends the person to get just a few things at first. Then, as they become faithful in getting the few things and doing what she asks, she will give a longer list and more responsibility based upon the level of trust that she continues to build through these small tests or experiences. In the same way, we gain trust with another person, bit by bit in our small actions, before we move on to the larger, more important actions. That is why it is so important for us to understand the importance of trust within our intimate relationships. We must cherish trust and we must not take trust for granted. If you can't grow to be open with a person and not hide anything, that is a relationship or a person that you need not attempt to be with. Trust is one of the first qualities that you want to look for. I also revert back to the spiritual relationship that we talked about earlier—if you are not bearing your all in your spiritual conversations with God, you need to evaluate your relationship. If your prayers are not open and honest about all you have done or all that you are feeling, there is something wrong with your relationship.

We have to learn how to deal with evaluating every relationship in our lives because they all affect each other. It's important to develop relationships fully, not just based on emotional desires, but on friendships and trust. When that physical attraction is gone, you will have to have something solid to hold the relationship together. You will get old, fat, skinny, bald, or you may one day wake up and not be able to function as you once did. You may have a stroke, be paralyzed, or dismembered, and the tests of your relationships will start. That is the time when we finally get to see what people really think about us and how people really care about us. What's unfortunate is that we wait too late to assess these things, and then realize that we have spent all of our lives trying to force ourselves to be with the wrong people.

The relationship between parents and children is very critical. I have already talked a little about how men / women relationships affect our children. Children are

very impressionable and also very observant. We try to
shield our children from many things in life, but we can
damage them so much when we try to hide things that
we don't understand or are embarrassed about. Most of
the time, the reason that we try to hide things from our
children is because *we* can't take them. Sometimes we
create untrue stories that we tell children to try and
explain or hide the truth from them. I mentioned earlier
how important the truth is in relationships. I cannot
stress that enough when talking about our relationships
with children. Sometimes, when we don't tell the truth,
we create a false reality. Then, when the truth is
revealed, it can be damaging because it affects a child's
ability to trust you after you have lied to them. Parents
and grownups are manipulated into believing that
children can't handle the truth. We are also damaged,

because when we were children someone believed that we couldn't handle the truth and now we are forced to question and compromise our whole way of thinking based upon one deception.

We have to learn to talk with our children and build the trust that is necessary in healthy relationships. We also have to allow our children to talk to us frankly and truthfully. We cannot ignore the warning signs that our children give us, the subtle signs that something is wrong or that there is something going on that they don't understand. We have to read each other's body language and know that we can trust each other.

We also have to become trustworthy in the relationship. Sometimes, we have to prove ourselves to our children.

Even though we are the adults and we may feel that we shouldn't have to explain or prove things to our children, there are times that we do need to, and we should. Isn't it funny how we feel that we are grown and our children shouldn't question us, but we turn right around and question God? Isn't it funny how we feel like we shouldn't have to explain to our children, but we feel like we have to have an explanation from God, even when he has given us the simplest and basic commandment to follow, "love one another, as he has loved us"?

We have to make our children feel safe enough and trust us enough to talk to us about everything. They will be introduced and exposed to things outside of our homes and our supervision; that is just how life is. We cannot protect our children and shield them from everything, but we can equip them with the knowledge and guidance needed to make the right decisions and understand the consequences of their actions and reactions. We can give them a better chance to make the right decision and feel good about it, when we share with them the mistakes that we made and acknowledge that we don't know everything and that we haven't been there before. We can equip them with the *love* that they need to understand that if they do what is right their parents will reward them and uphold them and celebrate them for doing what is right. Most of all, we can love them, and pay attention to their skills and talents, and help them develop their own dreams, and not force them to live out our failed dreams.

We can develop our relationships with our children, even if we can't get along as a couple or as parents of a child. There is always a common ground of respect that can be built for the sake of allowing our children to have their own shot at being successful in meeting the right person and acquiring the right friends. They can grow up and know that a friend is someone who won't encourage you to do wrong and join in unsafe activities. They can understand, by our actions, that a friend is someone that cares about you and your welfare and the consequences of your actions. Our children can be so much more equipped if we can learn to be fathers to our daughters and mothers to our sons. I know that there are so many single parent homes, and that many children only have single parent relationships. But a single parent relationship is better than no relationship. You know your faults better than anyone else does, but you also know that your child is a part of you and they are your responsibility. It is up to you, even if you feel you have been dealt a bad hand, to help your children avoid the same mistakes that you made; to overcome the faults that you have struggled with and may still continue to struggle with.

Too often, we leave our responsibility for our children to the wrong people. We expect too much out of the school systems, the government, and the world around us. If our children aren't learning, we want to blame it on the school or the district administration or the educational programs being used. We have a responsibility to teach our children and learn with our children so that they see that their parents are willing to do what they are asking them to go out in the world and do every day. We have to do more living than talking. We have to be better examples and show our children how to overcome poverty and adversity. We have to show them how to earn millions and how to appreciate what is theirs. We have to show them how to take care of themselves and their communities. Let them know that if they throw trash in their neighborhood, they will have to live and sleep with that same trash. They will have to eat that same trash and breathe that same trash. But if they take care of things, remain responsible, work toward success, they will reap positive rewards and create beauty and peace wherever they go and whatever they do.

We have to develop our relationships with our children and families in order to change our quality of living.

Sure, we have come a long way since yesterday, but we still have a long ways to go to avoid repeating the errors of yesterday. We must take care of today for a better future.

We have to develop *relationships* in order to change the peril that we are facing on the horizon of our future.

OMG! MY GOD, MY GOD

CHAPTER 6: MARRIAGE

Marriage is a sacred thing. It is the union of two individuals, one male one female. Marriage is something that should not be entered into lightly. It carries a tremendous responsibility. It is comparable to the body, as it pertains to functioning as a unit. If every part of the body doesn't work and perform together, you will find that nothing works at all. For each member of the body there is a responsibility. If my left arm is separated from my body or injured in some way, my whole body feels the pain of it not being there. However, my right arm doesn't get upset and start to remove itself from the body and say, "Well, if lefty is not here, then I'm not going to do anything to support the body either." Rather, it either continues to perform its function or it performs its function and compensates for the responsibilities of the missing left arm.

In this day and age, divorce is on the rise, and there are all kinds of reasons listed for the higher divorce rates. Money is one of those reasons. Infidelity is also another reason on the list. I mention divorce in this particular part of this chapter in order to use the analogy of the body and dismemberment or injury. Sometimes, people do not follow the basic examples that are given to them in life. If one person is not functioning in a marriage in the way the other one expects them to, sometimes the other person feels that gives them a right to act just as much a fool as the one they are disapproving of. I'm sorry, but I don't know of anything that actually works that way. When you are in a marriage, you are in a union. You are supposed to function as one. You are supposed to develop a working relationship that will allow you to be successful in developing a safe and healthy family.

It's of utmost importance that both parties have respect for the institution of marriage. Since the institution of marriage was set up by God, it's also important to have God's guidance to lead you into and through marriage. I look at marriage as an investment, and when you invest in something you have to do your research to be successful. It's important that you know the assets and the risks of your investment in a marriage, before you marry. Often, we are inclined to marry someone based simply on feelings. Yes, there will always be an anomaly where someone acted on impulse and everything turned out okay, but no one can continue to make life long decisions based upon impulses and just hope that it happens to work out.

Most of the time, when we enter into the stage of engagement or marriage, we have had to deal with some truths in regards to the person that we are contemplating joining our lives with. Truth be told, a lot of people are living out nightmares and impossible situations simply because they lied to themselves about some realities that were already evident. If the one you want to marry cheats on you prior to marriage, getting married is not going to solve the issue. The act of getting married doesn't solve those types of problems. People should marry because they love one another and want to spend the rest of their lives together—not marry to manipulate the other person into doing what they want or solving a problem in the relationship. If you have some concerns about other relationships or situations going on, it's important that you address those issues before joining in a union of matrimony.

There has to be honesty in any relationship for it to be successful. It's important to pay attention to how you are treated in this kind of a relationship because we do unto others as we would like to be done to. Whatever I will do to you, I will do to myself, whether it is something bad or something good. Many times we don't really pay attention to that part of a person's nature. It's really hard to admit that we do things to and for others in an attempt to silently say, "Hey this is how I want to be treated." You will find a good match in a relationship when you find someone who is willing to treat you like you treat them. It's important to pay particular attention to that.

We have to take a step back when going into a relationship and define what it is that we really want out of a marriage and a relationship. Mostly, we need to step back from what we have learned and what we know in order to decide exactly what "we" want out of a relationship. Often, we base our relationships on what we have been subjected to. We don't really take time to analyze and peel off the bad things that we have seen or been exposed to in all of the relationships around us. Each one of us can examine those relationships close to us and honestly say what we like and what we don't like as a personal preference; however, what we tend to do is accept the whole relationship whether bad or good, and then we look for the person that has those characteristics. We have been exposed to many different types of relationships through viewing the relationships of parents, grandparents, aunts and uncles, neighbors and even relationships that we've watched on television. We determine that if there is something that isn't what we want in our spouse or relationship, it is okay—as long as they have some of the good characteristics that we seek. In other words, we ignore things that we should pay attention to, in order to reap whatever benefit we want to reap from the relationship. Sometimes the benefit is financial security or sexual satisfaction or prestige and notoriety.

Today, we witness the vicious cycle that takes place in relationships when bad behavior such as verbal or physical abuse is tolerated because the abuser has some other good traits such as the ability to pay the bills and provide financial stability. The person being abused may say, "If this person can accommodate my physical needs, I will overlook their infidelity or lack of emotional commitment to me." We seem to think that it's okay to compromise in relationships and still be successful in the relationship. In mentioning this, I want to point out that just because someone doesn't meet all of the criteria, does not mean that you just throw it all away. We have to be able to communicate what it is that we want and also support that person being what we want them to be. This must be done before we make that lifelong commitment of marriage, though. If you start out right, most of the time you will end up right. This does not apply to someone who is cheating on you or abusing you, because there should be no tolerance for that in a relationship. Often, we miss the signals and the opportunities to communicate what it is that we want out of a relationship. Communication and understanding is what is essential to a successful courtship and marriage. We have to understand the underlying foundation of communication in our relationships.

We often assume that when we are with someone that they should know what we want. We assume that after a while they should know exactly what we want, and that's simply not always the case. It's important to open up and instruct a person on how to please you in all ways. We don't come with a book of instructions, so how can we expect for someone to just know what we like, what makes us tick or what floats our boat? That goes both ways. You can't be too proud to ask or to create a platform for instruction from your mate. This is all a part of researching your investment. When you are going to buy stock, first you research the company, what the company creates or manufactures, who the board of directors consists of, what their accomplishments are, and what this company or stock can do for you. All of these things can help you make a sound decision on where to put your money and what kind of return you might expect. Should you be any less concerned when it comes to the person you want to make a lifelong commitment with? Should you be any less careful? No— absolutely not.

Often, we don't spend enough time getting to know a person, spending time with them without being attached or involved sexually, doing a background check, knowing who their family is and how they behave. All of these things are really important to your success in a relationship. In regards to sex, if you live long enough there will be a time when you won't be able to enjoy that as you did when you were younger or as much as you would like. So, at that point, what do you have if your relationship is all physical and material? What do you have if you have not developed a strong relationship? If you don't have a well-rounded relationship that includes mental, physical and spiritual intimacy, you will find that your relationship doesn't have merit if you can no longer be physically involved. It's important to take the time to build your relationship on every level, not just on a physical level.

In a marriage, it is important to also learn how to enjoy your own individuality, but most importantly to learn how to live together as one. You have to learn how to function as a unit, but it is my opinion that you definitely also need to learn how to spend time apart. This is time that you take to exercise, shop, enjoy a movie, or even go on a trip. I find that when I am alone, I have times to think about the things that are going on in my life and how I really feel about them. It gives me a time to reflect on some of the things that I may have said or done that may or may not have been appropriate or may have been perceived in a way that I didn't intend. We really have to face the fact that, as individuals, we sometimes don't get our messages across the way we intend to because we really don't know the people in our relationships and their personalities, and how they function.

When we spend time alone, apart from the other person, it allows for a longing for the other person to develop. It is true that absence makes the heart grow fonder. A time of absence can make us appreciate the person we are in a relationship with, and we find that we truly do want to spend time with that person. I think that if you cannot spend time away from the one you are in a relationship with, and enjoy yourself while you are away, you really need to look at what kind of person you are and learn how to be content when you are alone. It's important that you can have fun and enjoy yourself on your own and with other people such as family, friends, co-workers, and society in general. This will increase your coping skills during times when you may experience a tragedy or loss in your social circle. It also builds the strength and character of any relationship, because you have developed thoughts and interests that you can share when you get back to the other person. Each partner in any relationship should learn how to respect and allow the other person to have the time that is necessary to spend doing something that is away from the relationship in order to develop personal growth. It is not healthy for one or both of the people in the relationship to be clingy and to only spend time together to the exclusion of ever being alone or spending time with other people.

Learning to live together is important in order to balance your relationship, as well. We are all individuals, but we do need help from each other. Why else would we have billions of people living in the world? We all need each other in some form or another, but tailoring it to the relationship, we need each other so that we can learn to survive and learn to survive in a better way. As an example, I perceive myself in one way, from my personality to the way that I look. Other people see me differently than I see myself. Sometimes, there are going to be some things on you or about you that you just won't be able to see, even if you have a mirror. Other people can see those things about you. You have to develop relationships with your friends, family, and most importantly your spouse, to be able to accept that view of yourself from them. Accepting constructive criticism is a must for any mature adult. When you develop these relationships and you are able to accept the constructive feedback offered by the people close to you who are privy of your habits and so forth, you are able to become a better, well-rounded person.

In marriage, you have to respect the other person and their opinion. When you join together in holy matrimony, truly there should be a common mindset of "us." You have to learn to discuss your financial situations and your decisions for the family with your husband or wife. Some of us like to say, "Well, this is *mine* and that's *yours*," but that is an attitude that is destructive and disastrous for any relationship.

You also have to consider the feelings of another person. It's not just you alone that counts. When I make spending decisions, for example, I make an effort to tell my wife what I plan on buying and why. The reason I do this is to give her an opportunity to help me with the decision of doing what is best for our family. What I mean by that is: I may be planning to buy something for leisure or pleasure, but she or my children may need something that I wasn't aware of. When I voice my desire to spend some money, that provides a chance for her to say "Honey, I don't think that's a wise decision and here is why." Or that allows her to say "Honey, the children need some new clothes and shoes, so I think we should wait a bit on your fun purchase." That allows me, the head of the household, to check the pulse of the family and make sure that I have first provided everything that the family needs before I make a decision without knowing what everyone needs. You have to keep the lines of communication open about everything. Communication is a core, fundamental key to your good relationship and marriage.

Even when you disagree, it is important to talk about things, so that you understand and respect why you disagree, and then you are able to come to a common ground in a respectful manner. Where people usually go wrong with keeping communication open is when they start to disrespect the other person and not put them on equal ground. There are people who are so adamant that their point of view is the only point of view and they try, sometimes even physically, to force the other person to see things their way. This is one example of what perpetuates domestic violence. One person is not willing to respect the other person and they want to beat their idea or way of thinking into a person. Being respectful and communicating are key components in a good relationship.

Creating goals and learning to work together as a team is really important, as well. How often are we taught in school and at work that the team concept is important? At work we are taught that the quality of our actions and work directly affect the success of our company or our employer. Why do we think that when we come home everything about team cooperation goes out the door? Our families and our marriages are a corporation or team of sorts. We have to build assets and make investments in our relationships, like we do our stock options.

One of the most difficult subjects that seems to make or break relationships is money. Often, there are little things and exercises that we can do to learn how to deal with adversities such as this very issue. It's very important to create a budget and to make plans on how to accomplish the financial goals that will lead to success in your family. Often, people come into relationships with bills or debts. Most people have some type of financial obstacles in their life. When you join in a marriage union, it is important to come together and make plans to tackle any financial situations that are there. You are joined as one, so whether you like it or not, what affects her affects him and vice versa. Both parties must be willing to handle finances in a way that is best for the marriage.

Take time to make a list of all of your bills, all of your needs and necessities, and make a budget for fun things. Also, it is important to plan for the unexpected. There will always be things that will come up unexpectedly, and if you are prepared for them they will not cause as much tension in your relationship. In addition to adding up all of your monthly expenses such as mortgage or rent, utilities, car payments, etc., you also have to add food, toiletries, snacks, cleaning supplies and things of this nature into your budget because they are a necessary part of your life. When you plan your spending, it helps to eliminate stress and the pressure that can destroy your relationship. It is hard to do this. I'm not saying that these tasks are easy to do. One of the hardest things in doing this is being honest and open about everything and admitting that you may have some problems with managing your assets and debts. Humility is so important in these instances because you have to be able to admit that you may or may not be the best at taking care of your own life. Once you can do that, you can take a step toward successful financial management. You can take these same steps toward any projects in your life. Things like remodeling the house, performing maintenance to the home, going on a trip, washing the clothes, and even cooking dinner can benefit your family and relationship if you are willing to work together and make plans to accomplish your goals.

The most important thing in a relationship is to have fun. You have got to learn to enjoy each other and each other's company. It's important to get to know your mate and your children all over again and again. Every day we change and we evolve. Some things that I enjoy today, I may not enjoy tomorrow. So, if we go through life thinking that we know a person based upon one or two conversations, we become outdated in our relationships because we are not aware of the changes in opinions and views that occur daily. Most importantly, every day is a *new day*. You can't change what happened yesterday, so it's important to live each day like a new day. Let the things of the past go and figure out how to avoid the same mistakes and obstacles in your relationship on a daily basis. We are actually too much like computers in some instances because we "save" everything that happens to us. We even do a "save as" on some things and label them and keep files and folders on them so we don't forget and forgive and move on. So, whenever that situation arises, we go back to our folders and react based upon what happened in the past. That's why you will find that you have some old and unhappy couples that will rehash every situation that could have happened 20 years ago, as though it happened yesterday. You will see people argue and act upon things that they carry in their hearts toward their mates, their families and even their children. We have to stop that type of behavior. After all, if you saved every E-mail and every document that comes across your desktop, you would reach capacity and then something has got to go or you would be stuck with the same old desktop. If you put this in perspective to your relationship, you will see that there are some things that you keep and some things that you absolutely have to let go. As a mature partner in a relationship, it is your responsibility to understand what should be let go of and what should remain to enhance and strengthen your relationship and help you grow closer to your partner.

CHAPTER 7: STDs (Sexually Transmitted Disease)

This chapter relates to an issue that has long bothered me and one that is becoming a growing problem in America and all over the world. There are numerous types of sexually transmitted diseases. These diseases can seriously affect not only your quality of life, but the quality of life for those around you. The symptoms of STDs can range from blindness to death. Some diseases that are in our community are man-made diseases and some have been introduced into the community through medical experiments. This is a disturbing thought; nevertheless, it is a reality. Now I could go on all day about the ideologies and the inhumane rationale as it pertains to the Tuskegee Experiment and the A.I.D.S.

experiments, but that would not stop the fact that it is out there in our community and it is taking lives of both the ones who are guilty and the ones who are innocent. I have seen the first hand effects of A.I.D.S., and I'm telling you that I would not wish that on my worst enemy, so it is hard for me to understand why someone would want to create something like this disease.

I want to reiterate the importance of responsibility. We all must take on the responsibility of educating ourselves and our children about STDs. In these times, we have to make education a reality and really push the concept of being responsible about sexual activity. Our culture perpetuates the idea of casual sex and the idea that there is no danger in having casual sex. In our culture and communities, people are conducting themselves as if there are no repercussions for casual sexual activity.

Sex is something that is a part of our lives because we are designed to reproduce like every other living organism on this earth, but we must emphasize the importance of the responsibility and consequences of being sexually active. It is no longer fool proof to have sex, even with protection, because there are so many situations where if those precautionary measures don't succeed, you could be on your way to your death bed. In my opinion, we still aren't concerned enough about our actions to provide a safe environment for our children and the generations to come. As I see it, we may be forced back to the days of courtship whether we like it or not. Our children will have to require their dates and suitors to take blood tests and be checked for STDs before they can even go out on dates. It only takes *one* time to contract these deadly diseases. It is becoming such a prevalent problem in our communities, and it's time to stop ignoring the issues and start taking the actions necessary to ensure that our children can enjoy life like we were able to.

Parents need to talk to their children when the children are at a young age, about sex and the STDs that can result from sexual activity. We need to show our children what A.I.D.S. can do to the body and how it can so drastically change someone's life and even lead to premature death. We need to start creating more community forums where we can reach our children and empower them to be able to enjoy a good and healthy way of life. There are many other diseases that are out

here that are affecting our children's health as well, but

A.I.D.S. and H.I.V. are currently ravaging and

destroying our communities. It is not safe to be sexually

active with multiple partners. It is not safe to be out there

creeping around or being open about being sexually

involved with multiple partners. We really need to be

prepared to search more thoroughly for our life partners.

We also have a responsibility to save our children by

educating them and providing them with the information

necessary to make the right decisions in every aspect of

their lives.

There are people in your family, in your communities, in

your churches, your synagogues, mosques, and temples

that have seen and felt the effects of H.I.V. and the

A.I.D.S. virus. We need to reach out to these people and

listen to their experiences and hear about their tragedies. We have to start taking care of what we have, and most importantly, each other. There are local clinics, Websites, and community centers where there is information available to educate our communities on these deadly and inhibiting diseases. If we each do our part, we can make a difference. We can see a change.

CHAPTER 8: HEALTH

I want to start this chapter by saying that this is an issue
that will be hard for me to discuss because it really hits
home with me as a man and especially as an African
American male. Our health is really important, and in an
effort to increase our success with dealing with health
issues I will have to share and shed some of the
ideologies that I possess in order to help everyone else.

Men, in general, don't like to go to the doctor or to the
hospital. I don't know a lot of people, men or women,
that like to go, but there is a strong resistance in the male
community to seek professional help with health
problems. Now, some of the reasons that I feel that we

are so reluctant is because we are *men*. While growing up and being taught how to become a man, one of the first things that boys are taught that is associated with being a man is that they must be tough and not cry. Boys are taught, in so many words and actions, that it is a sign of weakness to show that they are vulnerable and need help. Whether right or wrong, this is a sort of coming-of-age ritual for a lot of men. They are taught to be the stronger sex, and physically, men are designed to be able to handle a lot more physical pressure than women. In light of that kind of thinking, it goes unsaid that, in order to be a real man, males have to show that they are strong or unaffected even if they are really sick or even dying.

With these concepts in mind, I am attempting to explain the resistance that you will get from a man when you ask him to go to the doctor or the hospital. In our minds, we have been programmed that if we need physical help, we are weak. That mentality, I'm sure, has killed a lot of us or caused us to live in conditions that we probably wouldn't have to if we listened more to our families and loved ones. It is important that we monitor our health and that we address some of the stereotypes that we live with that keep us from living and enjoying healthier lives. It's tough and scary for a man to change that extreme way of thinking, because there is always that fear of your son not becoming the man that you want him to be or you worry that your son could grow up to be weak or feminine if you don't set an example of being tough. My opinion is that this is all a misconception, and that it is very important that men take a more active and involved role in the lives or their sons and other young men's lives. We have to start being more responsible men and better examples to our sons and the young men in our lives. We must be more communal in setting masculine examples for our youth and this includes our thinking about managing our health.

Concerning health, we have to dispel the myths and thinking that if you don't eat a hearty meal, you aren't a real man. This type of thinking is promoting overeating and unhealthy eating in our communities. This is directly affecting our health and our quality of life. There are so many stereotypes that have resulted in irresponsible behaviors in our communities. Also, by being so unhealthy and by following these misleading lifestyle ideas, we have created a society that is obsessed with characterizing and diagnosing every symptom that we have as some type of sickness. In general, people are quite paranoid that they are very sick, when usually they are not. A growing contribution to this paranoia is the advertisement of prescription drugs. When I was growing up, the only drugs that were advertised on television was aspirin or cold medicine. Now, we are bombarded daily with advertisements for drugs that are so strong, and sometimes potentially dangerous, that you cannot purchase them in the store and they cannot be offered to the general public. The drugs are so strong that they require a visit with the doctor and a prescription must be written for purchase of the drugs. This type of advertisement makes no sense. Why would I advertise a pizza on public television if you need a doctor's permission to get one?

Most of the drugs advertised have a list of symptoms that you can cross reference with just about every health related sickness known to man, and they all have an even longer list of side effects, some of which are worse than the symptoms that the drug is supposed to help. This is why it is important that we get concerned about our health, lifestyle, and habits, and learn to live in a way that is healthy instead of always depending on some sort of drug to put a bandage on our disease.

It is important that we educate ourselves more on our health conditions and get examinations as soon as problems occur. It is important that we read and seek information when we are experiencing any types of complications, whether or not we think they are just a minor issue. We have to learn to be more proactive when it comes to injuries or illness.

We need to start looking at prevention, and pay more attention to our bodies and learn what makes them run well and what makes them shut down. A lot of the pastimes that we enjoy, such as soft drinks and fast food, help to foster a lot of the health complications that plague our communities today. There are many children that are extremely overweight and experience sicknesses and conditions that are not normal for children to experience. Now, there is a trend where disease and sickness that used to be fatal only for matriarchs and patriarchs, is seen in infants, young children and teenagers. This is all due to our negligence and lack of education on how to treat our bodies and help them to run efficiently. We are just like most other machines. We need maintenance, a source of energy, a good washing and lubrication, and motion from time to time to make sure everything stays in good working condition. We should not expect to keep functioning in an optimum way when we ignore maintenance and care of our bodies. Most sickness and many diseases can be avoided if we take preventive care.

Once again, there are local health centers, Websites, and physical educations centers with the information available to help us in our desire to live more active and healthier lives. There is also nutritional information available to us about the food that we eat and buy. The law requires fast food establishments to provide the nutritional information on the labels or written literature on or with their meals. We have to take the responsibility to start paying more attention to what we are putting in our bodies and feeding our children. When we are not careful about living a healthy lifestyle, we are setting up our children to follow in our unhealthy ways. Do you want your children to suffer from diseases and sickness that can possibly be prevented with a healthy lifestyle and eating habits?

It is important that we implement some type of exercise into our daily activities. We have to stop being couch potatoes and sitting in front of the television waiting for them to feed us the information that we need in order to live healthy lives. We need to take our health seriously and seek out the information we need. We need to be proactive about good health for ourselves and our children. Get your family involved in some sort of physical exercise. It really helps to motivate you if you have a support group of people that are there with you when it is time to do those physical activities necessary to maintain a healthy life. Ride bikes together, go swimming together, play Frisbee™ or run races in the back yard, get the neighborhood children together for a game of softball or soccer at the park after dinner. There are many fun ways to incorporate exercise into your family time. If you pass these habits on to your children, it won't be so hard for them to make physical exercise and healthy eating a normal part of their daily lives, therefore eliminating the need to correct those harmful habits and behaviors that are causing so many of the health problems that adults and children are experiencing in today's world.

CHAPTER 9: EDUCATION

Education is so important to us that we really don't realize its significance as a whole. First, let me say that my mother was a teacher on several different levels so I realize the benefit of quality education. Education is a continuing thing. No matter how old you get, there is something that you can learn. We have to eliminate the stereotype that education is a chore and start thinking of it as an enjoyable experience. We need to help our children be excited about learning.

In our nation and communities, our teachers and educators are probably the most underpaid people in the job market. For the stress and preparation that it takes to educate and handle our children, we really need to make the changes that are necessary in order to pay our teachers more than they are paid. After all, they are more than just educators; they are also babysitters, counselors, and the people who have the ability to shape and mold our children.

Lately, I have seen some absolutely appalling things in my community. In the news, it has recently been reported that there was a threat to shut down all public schooling because of an issue with funding. More and more, I hear the stories of politicians campaigning that they will provide more funding for schools and provide a better quality education for our children. In the next month or so you could see that same politician is in the news for embezzling money or cheating on their taxes. There is no one looking out for our schools and our children in an adequate manner that makes me feel

secure that my children will continue to be provided the

opportunity to get a quality public education. This is an

issue that we must address on a local and global level to

ensure the protection of our future.

At the college level, tuition has increased at some

institutions to a level that eliminates the opportunity for

many of the less fortunate and monetarily challenged

citizens to provide continuing education for their

children. There are not enough programs that are

designed to help everyone. There are students that are in

college and doing well in their classrooms, but are

unable to pay the rising costs of tuition to stay in school,

while there are students on the Dean's list that are not

making the mark but are able to continue because they

are deemed financially challenged and they are receiving

assistance to pay for their college education. We have to create an even playing field and provide for those children that are making a valiant effort to get an education and make a positive impact on society through their education and being productive in their communities and businesses.

There are a lot of students that are not able to continue getting an education because they do not qualify as having certain financial or social disadvantages, and we have not provided an opportunity for those individuals that are making an effort to take responsibility by their educational actions and efforts to become a successful active contributor to our communities. My opinion is that education should be free for everyone, but I do realize that there is a cost to run these institutions. So we need to take a look at how to provide as many opportunities for those who are putting forth an effort and need assistance.

More and more, we are starting to realize that education for anyone but the wealthy is in jeopardy because of the ever rising costs of receiving a college education. It is also important that the universities and educational facilities take a closer look to make sure that equal opportunities are being given to each individual all the way down to the classroom levels. There needs to be a more grassroots approach taken to managing the structures and policies regarding the treatment of students. While there are some universities that have taken a proactive stand to allow minorities and financially challenged individuals to receive scholarships and provide an even playing field for a quality college education, these opportunities need to be provided on a more widespread and evenly distributed basis. Yes, there are some students that are forced to seek education at an institution that is less desirable, based upon the ranking of the school and the funding that the school receives. In order to create balance, you have to make some drastic corrections to get back on track.

We hear more people complaining that there is now reverse discrimination or unfair opportunities that are given to minorities and those that are financially challenged. As people and as a society, we eventually will have to face the fact that the years and years of limiting opportunities to minorities and those less fortunate is what is causing these situations to seem so unfair. Understand that for many years, minorities and people of color were required to pay taxes that contributed to supporting continuing educational opportunities for other people, but they were not allowed to attend the colleges and universities and were prevented from pursuing a higher education in order to become better and more productive citizens in the community. We have to acknowledge these injustices and be willing to compensate people with the opportunities to better themselves and receive the same opportunities to be successful and become a productive part of the society.

OMG! MY GOD, MY GOD

CHAPTER 10: RACISM

Racism is always a touchy and controversial subject and issue. However, I have to take a real approach to it, just as I have with all of the topics of all of the previous chapters. We can't deny that racism is present in our societies and in the world as we know it. We can't pretend that it is not around. We also have to face the fact that it is here and learn how to deal with the situations that arise from racial issues. Complaining about it and using it as an excuse for our short comings is no longer acceptable. There are great examples of pioneers and people who have endured and overcome racism, whether they will admit it or not, and still remained successful or accomplished their ambitions or goals. I have heard many stories of celebrities that have been faced with these adversities and still accelerated to the next level of success, in spite of the opposition.

One of the first things that we must acknowledge in any indifference toward people of another race, is ignorance. The word ignorance traditionally carries a negative connotation. Most people assume when someone says that they are ignorant that it means that they are stupid or a moron or something of that nature. Ignorance is very simply a *lack of information or understanding*. If you think about anything that you fear, the basic root of the fear is ignorance. I must admit that I have a fear of snakes, mainly because I don't know enough about them. I am simply uneducated about snakes and do not possess the necessary information on how to act when a snake is around or what the snake may do when I'm around. My natural reaction, because of my ignorance and lack of knowledge of snakes and how they operate, causes a certain behavior when I'm around them. I'm either going to run or try to destroy them the best way I know how. When I was younger running away from them was usually my reaction, but now that I am older and have a wife and children, I have to support the role of protector of my family, so in most cases, my instant reaction is to figure out a quick way to destroy the snake. Funny thing is, snakes destroy a lot of other things that the ladies in my household don't like. I live right next to a wooded area, so it's inevitable that there will be bugs and rodents that inhabit the area we live in. So, if you are following my example of something that God created that serves a purpose, you will see where I'm heading with my analogy. *There is a purpose for every living organism on this earth, and for every person on this earth.* Racism is ignorant of and ignores this fact. Racism says that "I" serve a purpose on this earth, but certain others don't belong here. Racism says that other people being here, lessens the importance of *me* being here. Racism fears that there isn't room on this planet for *all* of the people God created to function harmoniously together.

When we embrace ignorance, we embrace the fear that comes along with it, which causes us to act irrational at times. When it comes to racism, it mainly boils down to our ignorance about a person's culture or background that causes us to try to run away, fear, or destroy the things we are ignorant about and don't care to educate ourselves about. Because of this ignorance, there have been some reactionary natures and teachings that have been passed down for centuries about people of other cultures and races. Racism is documented as one of the most horrible visible reactions to the ignorance that human beings embrace. Some of the effects of racism survive in our business and social institutions even today, many years after we should have learned better. We can cry and make excuses that this is why we can't do certain things, but there is no excuse for not seeking another way around these racial situations of ignorance. There is no excuse for racism to exist or for any mistreatment of any person or living organism on this planet; after all none of us created anything in its original organic state. However, it is imperative that we understand the purpose of things on this planet as much as we possibly can—and especially understand our own purpose for being on this earth.

OMG! MY GOD, MY GOD

There have been some things that I thought (and hoped) we had overcome, such as public displays of ignorance and comments made on national television, as well as some heinous crimes committed and displayed publicly for the whole world to see. This very country, the Untied States of America, was built on the principles of racism, and that pendulum doesn't just swing one way. The truth is that the slavery of African American people by the hand of their perpetrators is atrocious and horrible, but some of the African people in the country were also responsible, to some degree, for the vulnerability of our ancestors to be captured and put on slave ships, causing the destruction of the rich and glorious history of Africa.

OMG! MY GOD, MY GOD

Today, we still see the effects of ignorance and racism in regards to the genocide and destruction of people in Rwanda, Sierra Leone, Kenya and many other places in Africa where ignorance and greed continue to destroy the moral fiber and standards that we have for each other as human beings. We have to continue to support efforts to spread the word about how embracing this type of ignorance can be so destructive and harmful. We have to take away the excuses that people have used to embrace ignorance, by providing education and a spotlight in the smallest corners of the world where racial injustices still survive.

I am not, by any means, providing an excuse for anyone to be racist. I am only offering a logical explanation of why people are bigots, racists, terrorists and persecutors of other people. It seems so unfortunate that in the age of such advanced technology, that the lack of education and information can perpetuate so much hatred and abuse. It is our responsibility to address these issues in a tactical and responsible manner. I had an experience where I overheard a person describe Section 8 housing as a place where poor people live that is usually a bad neighborhood and crime ridden. Through the comments made, the underlying tone was also where African American people might live. Before I could address the issue I saw an encouraging effort by an African American. He didn't react in a defensive manner or posture, but he proceeded to educate the individual that the stereotype that she was imparting to someone else was incorrect. It was done verbally and addressed out loud the same way that the information was disseminated, so that everyone else around did not have an excuse to be ignorant and perpetuate the ignorance that was presented. We have got to take a stand and educate people that we all bleed red blood just like the next person. We are created equal and we must commit to providing that luxury to everyone else.

OMG! MY GOD, MY GOD

CHAPTER 11: FATHER TO SON and MOTHER TO DAUGHTER

This chapter is really dedicated to the disservice that we do to our children because of our scars and our inabilities to successfully manage our relationships with members of the opposite sex. When I was coming up, there were a lot of stereotypical statements that circulated in our communities, such as *a good man is hard to find* and *all men are dogs*, etc. A lot of these stereotypes got started because of bad situations that a group of individuals experienced and agreed upon, although they weren't necessarily true. They still exist today and some are addressed in movies, plays, books, and even musical performances by various popular artists.

OMG! MY GOD, MY GOD

In my later teenage years, there were statements and stereotypes voiced by a lot of men that all women are b****es, hoes, tricks, gold diggers, chicken heads, etc. Once again, these images and opinions were perpetuated by a group of individuals that had a common opinion or could relate to similar experiences and they concluded that, in general, all women were this way. In some music, these statements were used to degrade and empower men that felt this way to reshape women's opinions of themselves, and change the way that some women carried themselves and respected themselves. In regards to women saying that "All Men Are Dogs," a lot of men changed their opinions of themselves and attempted to change the way they carried themselves and reacted to women, based upon those stereotypes.

OMG! MY GOD, MY GOD

The thing that strikes me as peculiar is that when people have bad relationships, they rarely look at themselves and the part they play in the relationship. They rarely examine the behaviors that got them in that situation or that bad relationship. Then they give it another try, using the same process they used before to try and find a good man or woman, never realizing that their practices are the root of the problems that they are experiencing. Insanity is sometimes defined as doing the same thing over and over again, expecting different results. It's funny how ignorance plays such a destructive role in our lives and our behaviors, and we insist on remaining ignorant in relationships, but want different results in the relationship.

OMG! MY GOD, MY GOD

This is the meat and potatoes of what I would like to say about relationships. A man knows how to raise a boy or show another man how to be a man. A woman knows how to show another woman or raise a girl to be a woman. I'm not stating that a woman cannot raise a male child or a man cannot raise a female child. What I'm saying is that there are both intentionally taught and silently taught characteristics that a child picks up as he or she is developing into the man or woman they will become. There are some things that I can attempt to show my daughters in regards to showing them how to be women, but the best thing I can teach them is how a man should treat them by respecting and taking care of their mother and treating them and every woman they see me interact with, with respect and dignity. Ultimately, they see and hear what I do more than what I say. I can say, "Don't let a man abuse you or take advantage of you." However, if my example is to abuse and take advantage of women, that is what I will teach my daughters. That is what they will look for in the man that they seek to develop a relationship with. The same thing goes for a woman and how she respects and treats a man in front of her daughters. If a woman allows a man to walk all over her or be disrespectful to her, the daughter will tolerate the same thing because that is the example that she has been shown. Parents must remember that actions speak louder than words. It's inevitable, especially with children. They do what they see more than what they are told.

I see a problem with the level of respect, as well as our concern for our children and their future relationships with people, especially when it comes to the father's and mother's relationship. If your relationship with your partner isn't working out, why is it necessary to present a tainted picture of the relationship to the children and have them believe that all men or all women are no good? While your partner may not live up to your standards or be compatible in a relationship with you, it doesn't mean that you should deprive them of being a supportive parent in the upbringing of the child. (The exception would be if the partner is abusive or is unable to responsibly and safely take care of the child.)

We have got to grow up as adults and learn how to provide a peaceful family relationship for our children; one that does not include putting down and talking negatively about the other parent, even if the other parent is no good. After all, the person you are talking about is the child's mother or father, and we all know what grownups do when you say something bad about our mothers or fathers. Why should it be any different for the parents of the child to degrade and demoralize the children's parents in front of them?

The truth is that a lot of times the reason a parent doesn't want to be around is because they aren't respected when they are around the other parent. If they weren't respected when they were in the relationship, they are even more likely to be disrespected after they have departed or been "kicked out" of the relationship.

Referring back to the previous chapter on marriage, you have to take into account all of the bad characteristics and warning signs that you saw when you were on the way to making a baby or two or three, that told you that this person wasn't the one for you. The fact is, no matter what choices or mistakes you make in your life, that's no reason to cheat your child out of having a peaceable life and experience with the person that played a part in bringing them into the world. We cannot continue to perpetuate the stereotypes and generalizations that taint our children's development and outlooks on becoming and co-existing with a man or woman.

The ills of a lot of broken families are lowered moral values, low self esteem, drug addiction, sexual addiction, homosexuality and feminine tendencies in some males, and a general lack of respect for other human beings. No matter how much I try to teach my daughters about being a lady, I still play like a man, talk like a man, walk like a man, and think like a man. No matter how much a woman tries to teach a boy about being a man, she still talks like a woman, plays like a woman, walks like a woman, and thinks like a woman. If our children learn from our examples, we must be concerned about the damages that occur when we try to teach them things from another gender perspective.

All of the points made in this chapter tie into the other points made in this book. If you don't do a good job at recognizing how to manage each aspect of your life, you end up destroying or tainting another aspect of your life that may even affect someone else's life. If we don't make better decisions and manage our responsibilities, our children suffer and are left to defend themselves in a tainted and cruel world, confused about everything that you ever taught them. Fathers, no matter what you feel about the mothers or women in your lives, don't taint your children's thoughts and beliefs by the comments and actions that you present to them for examples. Mothers, don't taint your children's thoughts or beliefs by the comments and actions that you show your children in upbringing and rearing. Respect yourself first, and other's will respect you.

CHAPTER 12: FAMILY

Family is often defined as a biological connection to a predecessor or person. While this is true and definitive in most every instance, there are some situations that I have experienced, and others have experienced, where there are deficiencies in a normal biological contributor that have caused us to seek out or develop bonds with someone who may not be related to us biologically, in order to fill that void or need in your life. Let's start this chapter with the biological family and then move on to what we might call the emotional family.

In most cultures, the biological family is something that we are taught to protect. It's the place where you receive your physical characteristics as well as your psychological attributes. There are a lot of lessons or habits that are passed down through your family that are taught as a structured rule and then there are *silent* teachings that family members pick up on as they grow up in the family. These are sometimes things that you learn from watching others that you consider your teachers or role models. Over the years, in my family, I learned that the protection of the family and its reputation is so crucial that sometimes providing an untruth is practiced to uphold the *portrayed image* of the family. When telling a lie, the first person you have to lie to is yourself, and once you have convinced yourself that this story or information is true, you must practice to deceive everyone else around you in order to make this lie seem to be the truth. In my experiences, I've found that, often, when we feel it's necessary to tell a lie to someone, it's really the individual that is concocting the lie that can't deal with the truth of the matter. The person that you intend to tell this story to in most cases can handle the truth a lot better than the lie because the truth really cannot be questioned. Sure, you can attempt to question it, but the truth contains facts and certainties that prove that it is, without a doubt, the truth. When a lie is told, the person that receives this information will process the information and either immediately question it or realize at a later time that things don't add up. When that happens, people's curiosity naturally causes them to investigate the information that they have, and something within the human spirit let's you know that things don't add up.

In the biological family there are a lot of people that have experienced living with lies. Sometimes this happens because someone simply thought that a child was too young to process certain information or that the child shouldn't know the truth. The reality of the situation may have been too horrible for the adult in charge to deal with, so they created an alternate version of what really happened. No matter the reasons, often lies become a part of a person's life and they may live with that lie for many years before they realize that things don't add up and the lie doesn't make sense. At that point, they may begin to investigate and find the truth. In some instances they may never find the truth. Sometimes, those who know the truth have passed on and the facts are taken to their grave with them by the time the younger family members start investigating what they have always been told.

As a child, I was taught that Columbus discovered America. The next part of that story is that he was greeted by the Indians (now, more respectfully known as Native Americans). Beyond that, the rest of the story is Columbus' story, told from *his* point of view. But in American schools, we have been taught the story as *history* that actually happened. It's funny how people can use words to deceptively make you believe something when the truth is right there in the information provided. I mean, really, how could Columbus *discover* a land when there are already people living on the land that he visited? Did he discover the land? No. He went to the land that was already inhabited

by Native Americans. And that's just one small example
of how untruths are propagated.

There are stories in our families that have passed on
from generation to generation that have misled many
people to believe that someone was a relative or that
someone else or some other situation caused the death of
a family member. There have been abuses, rapes,
murders, incest, and all sorts of ugly truths that have
been hidden by fictitious stories that eventually don't
make sense to someone once they stop and put all the
puzzle pieces together. It's unfortunate that this happens
because the person that you have concocted this story for
will eventually find out what the truth is and, depending
on how well grounded that person is or how emotionally
stable they are, they end up having to deal with the truth

eventually. In my opinion, it's better to give a person the truth up front and give them the rest of their lives to work through it, rather than let them live with a lie that they silently have to work out until they get the courage to question the truth and challenge everything they believe in. I've seen some of these lies destroy people and everything that they believed in, and I've also seen a person with the capability to deal with the truth even after they've been lied to for many years. That just lets you know that they would have been able to handle the truth all along.

A person looks to family for direction and support. A family should provide the nurturing and all that is needed for growth, stability and well being. Family is where you learn to deal with others and where you learn how to treat people. With your family, you should be allowed to shed your innocence and grow into the knowledge of the truth. From your family is where you learn your spiritual values and habits. Family is where you learn your manners and where you learn how to take care of those that will come after you. Your offspring, your predecessors, your very essence comes from your family.

As individuals, we sometimes don't recognize or acknowledge our responsibilities within the family to both support and be supported. There have been a lot of things that tear at the moral fiber of our families. Over time, there have been very violent and life changing tragedies that have torn at the very fiber of the African American families and this has caused us to create alternate ways of existing within a family. In the movie *The Color Purple*, we see a good example of everything that I've discussed above. In the end, the truth prevails and all of the lies and injustices that had been suffered still are not able to hide the truth and what is right. To some, this seems to be such an incredibly fabricated story, but for those who have experienced some of these situations, they are able to identify with the tragedy and pain in the portrait of what *The Color Purple* is about.

Slavery was a very dark and tragic epilogue of African American history and it was the very start of the destruction of the Black family and today we are still suffering from some of the tragedies that were inflicted on our people. The one thing that is most often a misconception and not talked about is that African people had a lot to do with allowing their own people to be ambushed, enslaved and captured. While this statement is not meant to shift the tragedies of slavery over to our own people, there were many human injustices that caused the unfortunate events of slavery and all of the people involved in supporting it and taking a part of it are all to blame for a collective injustice. The separation of families is one of the most tragic situations that one can experience. We have most recently seen the devastation of this when Hurricane Katrina destroyed homes and families in New Orleans and the lack of leadership perpetuated a situation that allowed many children to once again be separated from their families. The family is where we learn to treat others and where we grow to become contributing adults to our society. When the family is not present to support an individual you will see that there are alternate realities and situations that are created that can be both positive and negative.

This transitions us to our conversation about the *emotional* family. I believe that in the African American community it has been necessary to fill some of the voids created by historical tragedies and fill individual voids within the family with alternative people and groups, when mothers and fathers are absent or the family has been affected by drugs, poverty, disease, or religious views.

In the corporate world, the family is only taken in consideration if the family is considered to be the immediate biological family. So many times it is not understood that there was someone else that stood in the place of the normal mother or father. Sometimes, it's a grandparent, uncle or aunt, family friend or neighbor that has provided the "family" experience or nurturing for children. So when an aunt or uncle passes away, in many cases that person really stood in the place of the mom or dad and it is unfortunate that this experience is not understood or defined. Because parent replacement seems to happen most often in nationalities that experience poverty and other tragic lifestyles and events such as slavery, the corporate world seems to have little regard for the grief and bereavement of those affected, and little concern for health and mental care after such a loss takes place.

The family is something that is undeniably important in the individual life of every member of the human race. Many people who join gangs say that they did so out of a need to belong to someone or something, so they found a group of people who would fill that void in their life. They choose other people (gang members) who have also experienced a lack of family connection and belonging.

We often join organizations and social groups because we desire and need the collective family experience. We look for the support (both emotional and physical) of a group of people that will provide unconditional love. We have a basic need as human beings to belong to a group or a family of like-minded individuals. Many of us join external groups such as religious groups and organizations, as well as professional groups and organizations, seeking what we are looking for in our families.

When looking at our need to belong to these "families," it is important to set expectations of what our families should be for us, and to internally learn to support the family structure by understanding the roles of the family and each part of every family member. In the Christian belief system, the very basic family would be a husband and wife. The Bible speaks of the power of "two or three" touching and agreeing on the same thing. It says that God would be a power source of action in their midst. This is one religious view of looking at the family being interchangeable with the "two or three" explained in the idea. You can add children to that very basic family structure and continue to expand the family as you continue to add relatives or family members. This idea speaks very loudly to the importance of family in regards to this religious view. Understanding the original intents of the family as a support base can help us to understand how to get back to a normal family structure and function, eliminating some of the jaded or alternative experiences of family because of lack of responsibility, tragedy or loss.

With divorce and separation being a very big and sometimes tragic issue that many children have to deal with, it's important to allow, when possible, a healthy relationship with both parents even if the parents aren't able to live together or work out their relationship. Of course, in cases when safety is a concern, we have to responsibly consider those situations and manage them as they need to be managed. There are things that can only be taught to a boy or young man by a man, and many things that can only be taught to a girl or young woman by a woman. There are so many things that we don't take into account when our children are being raised. The information they process and all that they observe is very necessary for helping them to become healthy, loving and caring adults. It has been said that when you communicate, at least 50% of your communication is through your body language. As I have become an adult, I realize that the things that stuck with me most were the things that were taught to me silently. Most of the silent things taught were through body language. If I'm communicating to my son or someone else's son about how to be a man, it's safe to say that 50% of what he picks up from me will be my body language. My son will observe how I react to certain situations; how I treat women; how I conduct myself around the home. All of these things will come into play when things are being communicated from father to son or from uncle to nephew. These things are so important and we have a responsibility to learn our roles in the family and in the community, and to provide the proper examples to those that descend from us or those who are learning from us. If you are in a single parent home, it is important to provide your son or daughter with enough of the most positive examples and experiences of how to conduct themselves when it comes to gender, race, religion or whatever standards you want to set for them. Think about it—if 50% of communication is body language, a young son that lives with his mother and sees his father only 50% of the time or less, doesn't really have much opportunity for observing how to be a man.

This illustration should express how important it is for you to allow your child to see a positive example of someone who is well rounded in their life, family and social structure. If your child is only able to see his father or mother less than 50% of the time then that continues to respectively decrease the percentage of body language communication that they will get.

The family is an important institution and structure in our individual lives, and it is important that we preserve the family environment and structure in order to continue to produce great contributors to our society. Setting the right examples, providing the right level of hands-on support, as well as emotional support, will help to shape not only your children's futures, but it will enhance the quality of your future in regards to the family structure. Creating stories that are untrue or attempting to hide the truth from our children only increases the possibility of that same tragic event happening in the future. When we attempt to hide the truth, we keep people from understanding how these things happened in the first place.

In order to build strong families, we have to learn how to teach our children about finances, personal care, how to treat others, and all of the subjects that have been mentioned in this book. Learning how to speak to your children and help them to manage through their social and family experiences is one of the most important lessons that some people never learn. This causes them

to perpetuate the same mistakes and habits that continue

to keep individuals and families from growing and

prospering both physically and spiritually.

CHAPER 13: THUG LOVE

Thug Love…what a phenomenon! In my lifetime, I have seen this ideology taken to a genocidal level. I grew up in an era that marked the start of what would be called "Gangsta Rap," and while everyone is entitled to free speech and the freedom of expression and ideas, today's generation has taken this "thug" persona to a destructive level. I think being a "thug" is probably most attributed to Tupac Shakur, who was definitely one of the most talented people in my generation. There are many opinions, and there are some coincidences that seem to be very prevalent in the observation of his life and his actions. I actually had the pleasure of talking with Tupac over the phone after an interview that my college roommate did with him for the college radio station that he worked as DJ for back around 1992. We received his promotional copy of Trapped, which was a video single, and of course, we loved the song. This was his first solo effort, and we were well aware of his affiliation with Digital Underground. He was one of the most grounded and down to earth people that I could imagine, as I was only talking to him on the phone. He was excited about his career and he was so excited that we were really digging his music and that it was getting the airplay it deserved in a place the he didn't know much about, Lawrence Kansas. Tupac's career got off to a slow start, in my opinion, but then it just took off probably right around his role in *Juice*. I've heard that in acting that there are some roles that can be hard to shake when an actor is "getting into character." I would have to say that

OMG! MY GOD, MY GOD

I noticed some changes in the nature of Tupac Shakur when he played the role of Bishop in *Juice*. Personally, I don't think he ever stopped playing that role. I think that character took him over and he never let it go. Sure, he was a certified "thug," but when you listened to him, his "thugging" was originally about getting people out of a bad situation. It was about confronting poverty and making a better way for those that didn't have the same opportunities that were afforded the privileged in America. He was real about knowing what it was like to go without, whether it was food, money, a place to stay, a father, or whatever he felt that every human being should be entitled to. His original concept of being a "thug" has been so misconstrued because of some of the personal reactions and circumstances that he experienced, that the definition of being a "thug" or living the "thug life" transitioned into whatever Tupac was doing. Now, it has really gone to a level that I don't even think Tupac would be proud of. That's my opinion.

The funny thing about those that are trying to be like gangsters that are really only actors, is that they really have no concept of any of the unspoken rules and beliefs of the actual characters that they are trying to portray. In the movie, *The Godfather*, one of the most important issues for Marlon Brando's character was that he didn't want to be associated with cocaine and the physical ruin of the family by being associated with drugs. In the movie *Scarface*, Tony Montana who is played by Al Pacino, is all about a life of crime and doing anything he needs to in order to keep his money and power growing—that is until he's asked to assist in blowing up a car that contains a woman and her children. He had

limits and boundaries that he wasn't willing to cross. In

these examples, we see that even the so called "thugs"

have rules and things that they respect. However, a lot of

our youth grab hold of these characters and somehow

miss that there's at least some humanity to these

characters. They portray the characters without really

knowing them, based on what they see on the surface,

and they are destroying our communities and families

because they want to be "in character."

I have never been one to blame the music or the movies

for my behavior or anyone else's. I don't think that

music is responsible for killing or robbing or any of the

bad behaviors that people exhibit in the name of music

or movies. I just think that many people have a really

shallow mind. I grew up listening to all of the gangsta rap and I've seen some of the movies that have been blamed, probably hundreds of times, but that didn't make me run out to kill anyone or sell drugs or do any of the things I saw or heard in the movies. If there was anything I heard on a record that I did, it was because it was already in my head to do. Taking personal responsibility is a must for me. Some would say, "Well, look at the type of home you come from" or "Look at the opportunities that you had," but the truth is that there were times that I went without having my father around, and there were times that I went without. While it wasn't as bad as some other stories may be, I know what it's like to be without those things. I know what it's like to not have money for food. I know what it is like to be a few steps from homeless. It doesn't matter whether these situations are self inflicted or not; I have an idea of what it was like.

I take personal responsibility for my actions, and I know that I have to make my own decisions. While I know that there are some that aren't brought up that way, it's important for us to support an environment of accountability. Situations where things are haywire and chaotic can usually be linked back to people who are not accountable and responsible for their actions. We have to teach everyone to be accountable from a global level all the way down to an individual level. We are all linked together by our actions and our contributions to life. Every evil thing that we experience can be linked to an inability for someone to be accountable. Each situation reveals that someone didn't hold themselves or wasn't held accountable for their actions.

People must first learn to take responsibility, and then be accountable for the actions they take. By not taking responsibility as a world, a nation, a race, a community, a family, and an individual, we allow our actions to negatively affect everyone because we are not doing our part.

Being a "thug," by its original definition, shouldn't be a glamorous thing. Being destructive and irresponsible is always the easy way out of things. Selling death to someone's parents is not something that you're forcing them to do, but your hands are bloody as well if you are promoting such acts. If people are in a bad situation, providing them a way to destroy themselves is not the best way to help them. We all have come to a point and time in our lives where we were ready to give up on things and don't think rationally, but that gives us no excuse to take the "thug" exit and start to live a life of disregard, endangering those around us and the offspring that we helped to create.

I don't think you can really attribute the idea that Tupac had of being a "thug" or living the "thug life" to what is being represented in the streets these days. By no means does the true "thug" definition limit itself to one group of people or one particular race. There are corporate and government "thugs," as well, that need to be held accountable for their actions. Remember, our actions extend and reverberate past our individual circles and

197

affect more people than we care to think about. One definition I found defines a "thug" as a cruel or vicious ruffian, robber or murderer. So, there are a lot of groups, organizations, and governments that fit the bill for this definition. So while this term seems to be prevalent in certain communities and situations, know that if the shoe fits, we can put it on YOU!!!

CHAPTER 14: LIFE

Life is an interesting thing. It's a chance and an opportunity that is limited by time that we have no control over. We sometimes take life for granted, expecting every day that it will continue tomorrow. Most people don't practice living life like today is the last day. Of course, it sometimes seems ridiculous to expect tomorrow to be your last day on this earth, but it's a fact that if you knew you would die tomorrow, you would struggle with some of the toughest decisions of your life. It's inevitable that your life will end one day, but it seems that we continue to live life with the idea that death is never coming. We live life in denial that the inevitable day is coming when the air you breathe in

such an expected and familiar way will leave your body.
I think that if we truly had an understanding of life and
death, and a true perspective of it, we would live our
lives differently. The concept of living life like every day
is the last is so hard for us to grasp because we have so
many memories of all the past days, and we start to get
comfortable with believing that the memories that we
have of yesterday will continue to replenish themselves.
There are so many instances that have shown us that
tomorrow is not promised.

As I write, the human race prepares to cheat death and
the destruction or depletion of natural resources by
attempting to store away seeds of every plant life known
to man. We are attempting to make plans to live on other
planets aside from earth, and we've always experimented

with cryogenics and locking ourselves away in a capsule until things can be figured out. The fact is, we have mismanaged the earth and all of the things in it. We continue to live our lives believing that we can outsmart our Creator or what some would say is fate. We have all selfishly, in some way or another, abused a natural resource or opportunity to live another day.

Today, obesity is at an all time high in some of our societies. Over eating is a common practice in American society. Some diseases are at an epidemic level and are linked to our foods and social habits. We've destroyed clean water and natural resources on the earth in the name of luxury and comfort with our fancy gas burning cars and our use of plastic bags and bottles to carry our groceries and enjoy our favorite refreshing beverages.

OMG! MY GOD, MY GOD

We take life for granted, and yet, it is evident that we will have to take the responsibility and be accountable for how we manage our lives and the lives of those we are responsible for. Spending so much time planning war and other initiatives that have nothing to do with sustaining life, we continue to concentrate our efforts on things that don't perpetuate our survival or a better quality of life. Not only do we take no regard for our own lives, we also have no regard for the lives of others. We're distracted by the use of our cell phones when we are operating motor vehicles, with disregard for the power that our vehicle provides us in possibly destroying another life because we aren't paying attention to our driving.

OMG! MY GOD, MY GOD

There are bacteria and viruses that continue to attack human life, and we have seen the effects of things like the Bird Flu, Mad Cow disease and West Nile Virus. If you would really take the time to educate yourself and make yourself aware, you would see that there are many things that could happen to you daily that could greatly increase the chances of your death. There are a lot of things going against life. There is a lot of opposition to life and health. Of course, the objective is not to live your life in fear of everything, but to have a healthy respect for the gift of human life and take sensible actions to enjoy the time that we have left. Of course, you can't live your life in fear of everything, but by no means do most people have a healthy respect for the real odds that we ultimately will be destroyed by someone, something or our own selves.

OMG! MY GOD, MY GOD

As you read this book and consider all of the chapter titles, you can see that they are all seriously related to the outcome and quality of life. While we cannot control what we may call fate or the expiration date assigned to our life, there are so many things in our lives that we could manage much better, giving us at least a better quality of life. Sometimes, we need to take our life and manage it like a business. When considering the aspects of our lives, better planning and making better decisions could create a life that we could be satisfied with, and one that is without unnecessary disappointments and excessive horrible results. We need to take more time and effort correcting our mistakes and learning from them. We have to be willing to support each other, and to help others to enjoy a better quality of life.

CHAPTER 15: CONCLUSION

In conclusion, and in looking back over the previous chapters of this book, I must say that it took a long time to get to this point. Completion was a very tough point to reach. I hope that I was able to shed light on some things and share some experiences that may be enlightening to someone else. It took me a long while to get to the last chapter. I'm not what people may define as an expert on many of the topics that I've discussed in this book. What I do know is that I've had enough failures in my lifetime to write a book on nothing but that. I hope that some of my experiences have been enlightening, and I pray that the advice that started this endeavor was the right spark to this chapter in my life.

OMG! MY GOD, MY GOD

Looking back on things, maybe I should have forced myself to finish this book a lot sooner than I did. It came from my heart, so I wanted it to be real and not forced. I waited to be inspired and to feel like I was shedding what I believed to be helpful and enlightening. So many things have changed since I started writing this book that I could almost tear it up and start all over again. But I know that is not the right thing to do. It's all here on the paper now, and I feel honest and true about everything that I've said. My motivation and reasons for writing this book are pure.

I saw many faces, situations and circumstances when writing this book, and hope that my experiences and advice will clearly provide the spark in thought that people need to change situations in their lives. The bottom line is that you can't blame your actions or reactions on anyone else. You have to *own* your own actions and reactions. If someone does the wrong thing, it really doesn't provide an excuse for you not to do what is right. Remember, the truth is the truth and there's nothing that can prove it wrong. The real truth is what we seek every day, in every situation.

There have been many people, young and old, that I have wanted to share this book with and now I have the opportunity to do so. Once I have published this book and it is available, I hope that you will encourage someone else to purchase the book. I hope that it will be the spark of conversations and a new way of life and looking at things.

OMG! MY GOD, MY GOD

The one thing I know is that if you give people the tools to change things for the better, they will at least try it. We need more of our social and political figures to stand up and take responsibility for the message, music and examples that they are setting for our youth. We need for more corporations to take responsibility for the premises that their fortunes are built on. We need our leaders to fight with integrity and to take responsibility for their actions and the actions of others that they are responsible for. Until we make the changes necessary, we continue to perpetuate the destruction of the human race and we continue to degrade the quality of life that everyone enjoys around the world. The truth is that we all live in one big village and we all have a responsibility toward one another. Until we can make sure that every human being has a safe and comfortable way of life, our true reason for being here on this earth is never attained. Though you may pretend that you don't see the tragedy, poverty and injustices in the world, we are all partially responsible for each situation if we aren't doing something to contribute to a better life for everyone. We can change the world one person at a time. So, make sure that you take a little extra time to talk with our young people and help them to understand the truth about things. Don't get so caught up in your own life that you don't have time to spread some life and light to someone else. Remember, no matter what challenge or situation that you went through that may have been negative or destructive to you, someone helped YOU out and gave you a chance or provided something that helped you get where you are now. Someone helped you to go on to become what you are today. Provide those

same opportunities for someone else. LOVE…

www.ingramcontent.com/pod-product-compliance
Lightning Source LLC
Chambersburg PA
CBHW051825090426
42736CB00011B/1654